365 DEVOTIONS

POWER
MINUTES

FOR MEN

T0015705

365 DEVOTIONS
POWER MINUTES
FOR MEN

BARBOUR
PUBLISHING

Cover Design: Greg Jackson, Thinkpen Design

Published by Barbour Publishing, Inc., 1810 Barbour Drive, Uhrichsville, Ohio 44683, www.barbourbooks.com

Our mission is to inspire the world with the life-changing message of the Bible.

Member of the
Evangelical Christian
Publishers Association

Printed in the United States of America.

Guys, you've got a free minute now and then.
Guys, you need an occasional boost.
Guys, you should read
Power Minutes for Men!

Here are 365 brief daily devotions for guys of all ages. Each entry focuses on who God is. . . and what that means to you today.

Because He is powerful, He can help with any challenge you face.

Because He is loving, He wants the best for you.

Because He is wise, He'll always do the right thing.

Through both contemporary entries and "classics" from the likes of Charles Spurgeon, John Wesley, and D. L. Moody, *Power Minutes for Men* will provide the daily boost every Christian guy needs.

OUR LORD GOD OMNIPOTENT

And I heard as it were the voice of a great multitude, and as the voice of many waters, and as the voice of mighty thunderings, saying, Alleluia: for the Lord God omnipotent reigneth.

REVELATION 19:6 KJV

What better way to open a book called *Power Minutes* than with a reminder of the all-powerful God we serve?

"All-powerful" is the literal meaning of the term *omnipotent* found in this single verse in the King James Bible. The idea, however, appears all through scripture. We'll consider scores of related verses over the course of the coming year.

For today, simply know this: when you are part of God's family through faith in Jesus, you are covered and empowered by the ultimate force in the universe, "the Lord God omnipotent."

THREE IN ONE

"Therefore go and make disciples of all nations, baptizing them in the name of the Father and of the Son and of the Holy Spirit."

MATTHEW 28:19 NIV

God is mysterious in many ways, not the least of which is His unlimited power. But His "person" challenges our finite human minds as well. God is one God yet three distinct persons.

This year, as we consider who God is and what that means to us each day, remember that we are adopted by the Father in heaven when we believe by faith in the death, burial, and resurrection of His Son, Jesus. And then we become the actual dwelling place of God's Spirit, who empowers our Christian lives.

Understanding how God is three-in-one is less important than simply believing it—and believing that each member of the Trinity stands ready to help and bless you.

JESUS IS LORD

At the name of Jesus every knee should bow, in heaven and on earth and under the earth, and every tongue acknowledge that Jesus Christ is Lord.

PHILIPPIANS 2:10–11 NIV

Lots of people believe in God. That's a good thing. . .but it's only a starting point. Remember that the New Testament writer James said, "You believe that there is one God. Good! Even the demons believe that—and shudder" (2:19 NIV).

The next step—the most important thing—is belief in the life, death, and resurrection of Jesus. He is the way, the truth, and the life, the only access to God the Father. Why Jesus? Because He is the Father's beloved Son. Because He is one with the Father.

Every tongue that acknowledges Jesus as Lord does so "to the glory of God the Father." Why wait? Do that now, voluntarily and with pleasure.

CLASSICS: D. L. MOODY

GOD SEEKS YOU

*And the LORD God called unto Adam, and
said unto him, Where art thou?*

GENESIS 3:9 KJV

Adam ought to have been the first seeker. Adam ought to have gone up and down Eden crying: "My God, my God, where art Thou? I have sinned. I have fallen." But God, then, as now, took the place of the seeker.

No man, from the time Adam fell down to the present hour, ever thought of seeking God until God first sought for him.

"The Son of man is come to seek and to save that which was lost" (Luke 19:10). I believe the Son of Man who uttered those words is the same whose voice was heard back there in Eden, "Adam, where art thou?" For six thousand years God has been seeking man.

A POWERFUL HELPER

*May the God of hope fill you with all joy and peace
as you trust in him, so that you may overflow
with hope by the power of the Holy Spirit.*

ROMANS 15:13 NIV

Friendship, marriage, childbirth, and achievement are some of the many joys of life. But you don't have to be old to realize that life can be hard—sometimes very hard. God, however, offers us help in the person of His Holy Spirit.

The Spirit lives inside true followers of Jesus, convicting them of sin, reminding them of truth, growing the blessed "fruit of the Spirit" that makes this hard life livable, even beautiful: "love, joy, peace, forbearance, kindness, goodness, faithfulness, gentleness and self-control" (Galatians 5:22–23).

Through God's Spirit, we can even "overflow with hope." How does that sound?

THE RIGHTEOUS GOD

Then said I, Woe is me! for I am undone; because I am a man of unclean lips. . .for mine eyes have seen the King, the Lord of hosts.

ISAIAH 6:5 KJV

When we seriously consider our own lives, the amount of sin and ugliness we find can be overwhelming. And if we compare our own righteousness to God's, we might suddenly be filled with the urge to shrink away in shame.

Isaiah felt this self-loathing when he encountered God's glory in a vision. But instead of destroying the prophet with His power, God recognized Isaiah's humility and repentance and cleansed him of his sins.

The parallel between Isaiah's experience and our own today is striking. We stand in God's presence each day, deserving His wrath but receiving His grace. Because of Jesus Christ's sacrifice, our Father says to us, "Thine iniquity is taken away, and thy sin purged" (Isaiah 6:7 KJV). What a reason to rejoice!

THE GOD OF HOPE

The hand of the LORD was on me, and he brought me out by the Spirit of the LORD and set me in the middle of a valley; it was full of bones. He led me back and forth among them, and I saw a great many bones on the floor of the valley, bones that were very dry. He asked me, "Son of man, can these bones live?" I said, "Sovereign LORD, you alone know."

EZEKIEL 37:1–3 NIV

With every passing day, our world seems to look a little more like Ezekiel's valley of dry bones. Broken hearts and broken dreams snap beneath our feet, even as we try our best to tread softly among the lives of those around us. It's easy to lose hope.

But God desires to give us a future and a hope, and that hope is found in His Word. When scripture is alive in our hearts, we can speak to those dry bones today, and they will live again. That is the power of our God.

CLASSICS: MATTHEW HENRY

NOT ACCORDING TO OUR SINS

And I will establish my covenant with you, neither shall all flesh be cut off any more by the waters of a flood; neither shall there any more be a flood to destroy the earth.

GENESIS 9:11 KJV

God had drowned the world once, and still it was as filthy and provoking as ever, and God foresaw the wickedness of it, and yet promised He would never drown it any more; for He deals not with us according to our sins. It is owing to God's goodness and faithfulness, not to any reformation of the world, that it has not often been deluged and that it is not deluged now. As the old world was ruined to be a monument of justice, so this world remains to this day, a monument of mercy, according to the oath of God, that the waters of Noah should no more return to cover the earth.

RECOGNIZE GOD'S GOODNESS

*With praise and thanks, they sang
this song to the Lord: "He is so good!"*

EZRA 3:11 NLT

As a Christian, you instinctively know God is good. He created all you see. . .and don't see. From mountains to air, oceans to wind, we are surrounded by compelling evidence of a good God. He can be worshipped and praised, and He is the subject of joyful songs.

When gratitude bubbles up in your mind, let it also pour over your lips. Go ahead—express your heart to the God who is, in fact, *good*.

Something about recognizing God's goodness expands trust and widens perspective. It doesn't hold us back but frees our hearts to fly. Within the truth of God's goodness, our praise blends with gratitude. . . and changes the course of tomorrow.

If it seems like you don't have enough time to recognize God's goodness, perhaps you're spending too much time recognizing other things. Never forget how far He has brought you.

A CREATIVE GOD

In the beginning God created the heaven and the earth.

GENESIS 1:1 KJV

What's the first thing we can know about God from the Bible? If you open at the beginning of the Old Testament, you'll learn that God is creative. He made everything we see—and everything we don't—out of nothing but His power and creativity.

Keep reading the book of Genesis, and you'll discover that God made humans in His image, which means you were created to be creative too!

Each time you draw a picture, write a story, build a bookcase, make an omelet, or assemble an engine, you are living your God-given identity as a creator. The joy of creating something that didn't previously exist gives us a glimpse into the joy God felt when He created the heaven and the earth. . .and you.

What can you create today to capture that joy for yourself?

JESUS WILL RETURN

If anyone builds on this foundation using gold, silver, costly stones, wood, hay or straw, their work will be shown for what it is, because the Day will bring it to light.

1 CORINTHIANS 3:12–13 NIV

What does the apostle Paul mean by "the Day"? This is a classic shorthand phrase he uses sixteen times. In 1 Corinthians, we find the core truth of "the Day" early: "as you eagerly wait for our Lord Jesus Christ to be revealed. He will also keep you firm to the end, so that you will be blameless on the day of our Lord Jesus Christ" (1 Corinthians 1:7–8 NIV).

In other words, "the Day" refers to the return, revelation, and second coming of the Lord Jesus Christ for judgment. It includes the culmination of salvation and rewards for God's people.

Of course, some of that meaning comes from the immediate context, especially nearby 1 Corinthians 3:10–15 and 1 Corinthians 4:5.

What a day it will be. It should energize us!

FIND TIME TO BE ALONE WITH GOD

And he said unto them, Come ye yourselves apart into a desert place, and rest a while: for there were many coming and going, and they had no leisure so much as to eat.

MARK 6:31 KJV

In His life of secret prayer, my Savior is my example. He could not maintain the heavenly life in His soul without continually separating Himself from man and communing with His Father.

With the heavenly life in me, it is not otherwise: it has the same need of entire separation from man, the need not only of single moments but of time enough for intercourse with the Fountain of Life, the Father in heaven. . . .

If thou and I would be like Jesus, we must especially contemplate Jesus praying alone in the wilderness. There is the secret of His wonderful life. What He did and spoke to man was first spoken and lived through with the Father. . . . Even though it cost the sacrifice of night rest, of business, of intercourse with friends, the time must be found to be alone with the Father.

GOD GIVES NEW LIFE

"Rebellion and revolt are normal there!"

EZRA 4:19 NLT

A king analyzed the foreigners who had been brought into his kingdom and found ample evidence to convict the people of revolt and disobedience. The king sought the records and concluded that when the people had a chance to obey, they did the opposite. When they had the chance to honor, they chose disrespect. When they could have chosen wisdom, they opted for personal opinion.

If the same analytics were applied to you, how would you rank? Would the report come back "Rebellion and revolt are normal"? Yet God, the One who creates, loves, and forgives, stepped into the rebellion and shouted, "Redeemed!" He stepped into the sin and cried, "Forgiven!" He stood in the midst of hate and everything about His life spoke, "I love you."

Listen and respond, and God will take your rebellion in trade for His new life.

GOD'S KIND OF LOVE

*Love is kind. Love is not jealous. Love does
not put itself up as being important.*

1 CORINTHIANS 13:4 NLV

In other words, here is what love is like: God's kind of love. It's patient. It can wait. It helps others, even if they never find out who assisted them. Love doesn't look for greener pastures. Love doesn't boast. It doesn't try to build itself up to be something it isn't.

Love doesn't act in a loose, immoral way. It doesn't seek to take but willingly gives. Love doesn't lose its temper. It doesn't keep changing its mind. Love doesn't think about how difficult the other person is and certainly doesn't think of how it could get back at someone. Love is grieved deeply over the evil in this world but rejoices over truth.

Love perseveres, even when everything goes wrong and the feelings leave and the other person doesn't seem wonderful anymore.

That's what God's kind of love is like.

GOD WANTS TO BE KNOWN

The men who spoke for God were with them and helped them.

EZRA 5:2 NLV

Prophets were men and women who received messages from God and shared them with the people. The version used for today's scripture describes these messengers as "men who spoke for God." That is exactly what they did.

Think about this: if the prophets spoke for God, then God must have been speaking to them. They simply obeyed by telling others what they knew to be true because God had made that truth known.

This is the God you can serve. He wants you to know truth, and He's given you His Word as truth. He is a God who wants to be known and shared with others.

God doesn't leave you to wonder if you're getting it right. His instruction manual contains everything you need to know about life and godliness. Soak it in, then help others to understand it too.

CLASSICS: CHARLES H. SPURGEON

MERCY IS THE LISTENER

And the angel of the Lord said unto her, Behold, thou art with child and shalt bear a son, and shalt call his name Ishmael; because the Lord hath heard thy affliction.

GENESIS 16:11 KJV

Although there was no prayer of [Hagar's] for God to hear, another voice spake in His ear. The angel who suddenly appeared to her said, "The Lord hath heard thy affliction." That is a very beautiful sentence. Thou hast not prayed: thou hast been willful, reckless, and at last despairing, and therefore thou hast not cried unto the Lord. But thy deep sorrow has cried to Him. Thou art oppressed, and the Lord has undertaken for thee. Thou art suffering heavily, and God, the All-pitiful, has heard thy affliction. Grief has an eloquent voice when mercy is the listener. Woe has a plea which goodness cannot resist. Though sorrow and woe ought to be attended with prayer, yet even when supplication is not offered, the heart of God is moved by misery itself.

THE LORD WORKS IN MEN'S HEARTS

Praise be to the Lord, the God of our ancestors, who has put it into the king's heart to bring honor to the house of the Lord in Jerusalem in this way.

EZRA 7:27 NIV

A foreign king gave the signal for the temple in Jerusalem to be rebuilt. He drafted laws and put the full force of his authority behind their implementation. There were no legal threats to the king that made him do this. It was the hand of a God the king didn't fully understand but chose to honor.

Ezra understood that God gave this king the seed of a divine idea. God laid it on the king's heart to do something that, to some, made no sense. Sure, it made sense to show gratitude to the king, but it made more sense to praise the God who set things in motion for this reconstruction project.

God is at work in your life too. You might not always be aware of how, but good things can happen when you welcome God to offer a solution.

A MASTER CRAFTSMAN

God saw all that He had made and it was very good.
There was evening and there was morning, the sixth day.

GENESIS 1:31 NLV

After creating everything—light and dark, land and sea, sun, moon and stars, trees and flowers, all the animals, and, finally, people—God looked at His work and declared it to be "very good."

God didn't slap together reality as we know it and say, "Well, it looks good from the road." He didn't cut corners or use second-rate materials. God, who understands perfection intimately, didn't make things "good enough." He made them *very* good.

When you are tempted to cut corners, gloss over your mistakes, or rest when things are simply good enough, remember whose image you were made in. God made you to be very good, and the work you do should be held to no less than His standard.

GOD'S CALL TO RADICAL OBEDIENCE

"Now, son of man, take a block of clay, put it in front of you and draw the city of Jerusalem on it. Then lay siege to it: Erect siege works against it, build a ramp up to it, set up camps against it and put battering rams around it. . . . It will be under siege, and you shall besiege it. This will be a sign to the people of Israel."

EZEKIEL 4:1–3 NIV

Today, as in Ezekiel's day, God has a message for His children. And to deliver that message, He needs men who are willing to adopt an attitude of radical obedience.

Much as He did with Ezekiel, God called Isaiah to a radical level of obedience when He commanded him to walk naked and barefoot as a sign of the troubles that would befall Egypt if the people refused to repent (see Isaiah 20:1–3).

Are we willing today to embrace this level of radical obedience to bring the message of Jesus Christ to the lost and dying world all around us?

CLASSICS: ANDREW MURRAY

JESUS IS WITH YOU, ON YOU, IN YOU

*But the Spirit of the Lord came upon
Gideon, and he blew a trumpet.*

JUDGES 6:34 KJV

We read in Judges, "The Spirit of the Lord clothed Gideon." But you know that there is in the New Testament an equally wonderful text, where we read, "Put on the Lord Jesus Christ," that is, clothe yourself with Christ Jesus. And what does that mean? It does not only mean, by imputation of righteousness outside of me, but to clothe myself with the living character of the living Christ, with the living love of the living Christ.

Put on the Lord Jesus. Oh! What a work. I cannot do it unless I believe and understand that He whom I have to put on is as a garment covering my whole being. I have to put on a living Christ who has said, "Lo, I am with you all the days." Just draw the folds closer round you of that robe of light with which Christ would array you. Just come and acknowledge that Christ is with you, on you, in you. Oh, put Him on!

A PROFOUNDLY MERCIFUL GOD

"Now we are being punished because of our wickedness and our great guilt. But we have actually been punished for less than we deserve, for you, our God, have allowed some of us to survive as a remnant."

EZRA 9:13 NLT

The Lord is a merciful God. He cannot tolerate sin, but because of His great mercy, we humans can survive His justice. Mercy means not receiving at least some of the penalty for our sin, even though we are guilty before a holy God. If sin is common to all men, then mercy must also be common to a good God.

Ezra lived in a time of great wickedness and profound guilt. Yet, in His mercy, God worked in this environment to begin the process of bringing His people back from a time of exile.

God had corrected His people, and now He was restoring them—just as He does today. All we need to do is respond to His mercy by turning to Him in confession and repentance.

A GOD WORTH FOLLOWING

*Therefore, my beloved brethren, be ye stedfast, unmoveable,
always abounding in the work of the Lord, forasmuch as
ye know that your labour is not in vain in the Lord.*

1 CORINTHIANS 15:58 KJV

Throughout 1 Corinthians 15, Paul already has used the word *vain* five times. This is the sixth. Why is Paul stressing the need for "steadfast, unmoveable, always abounding" work for the Lord? Why is he saying that the Lord rewards such labor? Maybe, just maybe, because everyone is tempted to give up and quit.

What is the single greatest warning in the Gospels and Acts? In the New Testament letters from Romans to Jude? Even in the book of Revelation? Keep following the Lord—endure to the end—don't fall away. He is more than worthy and the rewards are oh-so-sweet!

GOD IS UTTERLY UNIQUE

"Sovereign Lord, you have begun to show to your servant your greatness and your strong hand. For what god is there in heaven or on earth who can do the deeds and mighty works you do?"

DEUTERONOMY 3:24 NIV

To those of us who know Him personally, the uniqueness of God is obvious. But one man, Moses, may have had the clearest perspective of all people. God spoke to him "face to face, as one speaks to a friend" (Exodus 33:11 NIV).

God had first communicated to Moses through a burning bush that was never consumed (Exodus 3). The Lord had performed numerous miracles through Moses and his brother, Aaron, in breaking the Israelites out of their slavery in Egypt (Exodus 4–12). Then God used Moses to part the Red Sea, providing escape for His people and death for the pursuing Egyptian army (Exodus 14).

So when Moses asked, "What god is there in heaven or on earth who can do the deeds and mighty works you do?" he already knew the answer. There is none. And none that can even try to compete.

Our God is utterly unique. And, Christian, He's on your side!

GOD DIRECTS OUTCOMES

And it came to pass, when I heard these words,
that I sat down and wept, and mourned certain days,
and fasted, and prayed before the God of heaven.

NEHEMIAH 1:4 KJV

As a resident of this world, you know bad news is often a part of life. Perhaps, like Nehemiah, you respond to bad news by sitting down and weeping—your heart has been broken over the bad news that runs through your mind.

An exiled Israelite, Nehemiah lived in impressive, secure surroundings. His life wasn't in danger. Yet he was aware of bad news regarding his true homeland. At that moment, he had no authority to step in and help, but he knew help was needed. The story told in the book of Nehemiah would have an entirely different ending had Nehemiah not stepped up in prayer and asked God for help.

The bad news you receive today will not take God by surprise or limit His ability to direct the outcome. So pray, and see what He tells you to do.

CLASSICS: ANDREW MURRAY

THE WORK GOD ALONE CAN DO

*And the Lord visited Sarah as he had said,
and the Lord did unto Sarah as he had spoken.*

GENESIS 21:1 KJV

One great cause of the weakness of the spiritual life of earnest Christians, notwithstanding their prayers and efforts, is that they seek to do the work God alone can do. They know not that God, whose Spirit dwells in us, will maintain our life in a divine power, working in us that which is pleasing in His sight. If they knew this aright, they would see that their one duty was in utter helplessness, in deep humility and dependence, to wait upon God and to trust and count upon Him to do His blessed work.

It is this Sarah teaches us. She knew what God had promised. For twenty-five long years her heart yearned for the son of whom God had spoken. At times her faith was sorely tried, but she ever came back to this one thing: He is faithful that promised! And in due time God did His omnipotent quickening work, and Sarah received power to become the mother of Isaac and of Jesus.

THE GOD WHO REWARDS PERSISTENCE

And ye shall seek me, and find me, when ye shall search for me with all your heart.

JEREMIAH 29:13 KJV

Have you ever been hopelessly lost? Maybe you took a wrong turn in the big city, or perhaps you lost your way while hiking a forest trail. No matter how old you are, being lost can be scary.

Faith can sometimes feel the same way. This world is a jungle teeming with contradictory voices and views, all striving for our attention. Amid the chaos, how can we ever find our way?

Well, we can't. . .not on our own, at least. Thankfully, God has the solution: "I will put my law in their inward parts, and write it in their hearts" (Jeremiah 31:33 KJV). Those who are indifferent or even hostile toward spiritual things may never notice the Holy Spirit's gentle pull. But those who eagerly search for God, like a lost child calling for his parent, will surely find Him.

A TRUSTWORTHY GOD

[Nehemiah] answered them by saying, "The God of heaven will give us success. We his servants will start rebuilding."

NEHEMIAH 2:20 NIV

God never promised that you can know the outcome of obedience ahead of time. Others may believe you are foolish for obeying God when you don't know how things will turn out. You may even find yourself questioning your decision to do what He tells you.

But God is 100 percent trustworthy. He doesn't condemn you to be the object of some divine joke. He has good plans for all who follow Him faithfully. That includes Nehemiah, who trusted the Lord and followed His plan, despite opposition that easily could have distracted him.

Surrender to God, not your fear. Trust His direction, not your anxiety over how things will turn out. Follow His guidance, not your own imperfect plans.

CLASSICS: ANDREW MURRAY

HUMILITY PLEASES GOD

*Even as the Son of man came not to be ministered unto,
but to minister, and to give his life a ransom for many.*

MATTHEW 20:28 KJV

Jesus brought humility from heaven to us. It was humility that brought Him to earth, or He never would have come. In full accordance with this, just as Christ became a man in this divine humility, so His whole life was marked by it. He might have chosen another form in which to appear; He might have come in the form of a king, but He chose the form of a servant. He made Himself of no reputation; He emptied Himself; He spoke, and His life confirmed what He said, "I am among you as one that serveth.". . .

Beloved, the life of Jesus upon earth was a life of the deepest humility. It was this gave His life its worth and beauty in God's sight. And then His death—His death was an exhibition of unparalleled humility. "He humbled Himself, and became obedient unto death, even the death of the cross."

GOD'S SACRIFICIAL CLOTHING

*And the Lord God made clothing from
animal skins for Adam and his wife.*

GENESIS 3:21 NLT

After Adam and Eve sinned, they had to leave the garden of Eden—but God didn't send them out empty-handed. Instead, He made clothing from animal skins for them so they could fare better in the outside world.

Making clothes from animal skins is intensive, time-consuming work. And it requires an animal to be sacrificed in the effort. Though Adam and Eve had broken God's rules, He showed them love by making such a sacrifice.

When you sin, life cannot go on as it did before. But God won't stop loving you. In fact, He's made the ultimate sacrifice by sending His Son to clothe you in His righteousness! As Adam was clothed by God's love to live in a broken world, so are you clothed by His love in anticipation of a perfect world to come.

GOD FIGHTS FOR HIS PEOPLE

Our God shall fight for us.
NEHEMIAH 4:20 KJV

God will never leave you defenseless against your enemies or against this world's opposition. He gives you everything you need to overcome and do things He has for you to do and to arrive at the place He wants you to be.

God had given Nehemiah the assignment of rebuilding the wall around the city of Jerusalem. He gave Nehemiah the idea to rebuild the walls, and He provided what was needed to perform the work.

Nehemiah faced opposition, but he stood firm and didn't run away. He was convinced God would fight a battle he could never win on his own. The Lord helped Nehemiah withstand the opposition from those who preferred that Jerusalem remain in ruins.

God fought for Nehemiah, and He can fight for you too. Your part is to make sure you are committed to obedience to what He asks you to do.

GOD'S LAMP

My people are destroyed for lack of knowledge.
HOSEA 4:6 KJV

We live in a world with an almost endless supply of information. Whatever we want or need to know, from the number of stars in the sky to the quickest way around the traffic ahead of us, is available right at our fingertips.

To live a powerful life of faith, God has given us everything we need to know—and all this information is available in the pages of scripture. That is what the apostle Paul meant when he wrote, "All Scripture is God-breathed and is useful for teaching, rebuking, correcting and training in righteousness" (2 Timothy 3:16 NIV).

In our daily war with this world's wisdom, let's remember to make God's Word our basis of knowledge. . .and the lamp that lights the path ahead of us.

CLASSICS: CHARLES H. SPURGEON

THOSE WHO WAIT UPON THE LORD

And thou saidst, I will surely do thee good, and make thy seed as the sand of the sea, which cannot be numbered for multitude.

GENESIS 32:12 KJV

The possession of a God, or the non-possession of a God, makes the greatest possible difference between man and man. Esau is a princely being, but he is "a profane person." Jacob is a weak, fallible, frail creature, but he has a God. Have you not heard of "the mighty God of Jacob"? There are many wise, careful, prudent men of the world who have no God; and truly these in the highest sense, like the young lions, do lack and suffer hunger; for their highest nature is left to famish. Those who wait upon the Lord are often very simple and devoid of ability and policy, but they shall not lack any good thing: their highest nature is well supplied from heavenly sources.

GOD AS OUR SOURCE OF STRENGTH

O God, strengthen my hands.

NEHEMIAH 6:9 NLV

When you feel overwhelmed—and everyone does at times—you should remember that the Bible is filled with stories of people who came to the end of what they could handle and called out to God for help.

When you know God wants you to do something, it's not a bad idea to pray the prayer found in today's scripture. The Lord can replace your weakness with strength, your timidity with confidence, and your fear with courage.

You can't do it all. You can't rely on yourself. When you need help, ask the One who can give it. You may have friends who can walk with you through difficult moments, just like Nehemiah did. But still he prayed, "O God, strengthen my hands."

God heard Nehemiah's prayer—and He was happy to give him what he needed. He'll do the same for you.

GOD ALREADY KNOWS

Now Cain said to his brother Abel, "Let's go out to the field."
While they were in the field, Cain attacked his brother Abel
and killed him. Then the LORD said to Cain, "Where is your
brother Abel?" "I don't know," he replied. "Am I my brother's
keeper?" The LORD said, "What have you done? Listen! Your
brother's blood cries out to me from the ground."

GENESIS 4:8–10 NIV

When a father enters his child's room, sees drawings on the wall and a marker in the child's hand, he doesn't need to be omniscient—all-knowing—to realize what happened. The father's question, "What have you done?" isn't a fact-finding mission; it's an invitation to confess.

After Cain murdered his brother, Abel, God already knew what had happened—and He invited Cain to confess his sins. Instead, Cain pretended not to know what God was talking about.

When you have sin in your life, feigning ignorance will only make matters worse. God desires honesty, even when our actions seem unforgivable. His love is always greater than our sin!

A PROMISE-KEEPING GOD

*"You have done what you promised,
for you are always true to your word."*

NEHEMIAH 9:8 NLT

In today's scripture, Nehemiah observes the wonderful truth that God keeps promises. He is always true to His word. That's an important truth that each of us should grasp today.

When God makes a promise, He never fails to keep it. He'll never be too busy or distracted to do what He has promised to perform. He doesn't need to sign a contract because His spoken promises are unbreakable, universal, and uncompromising. He will never change terms, downgrade His response, or create a breach of trust.

Even the best of us don't always keep our promises perfectly. But God does. The Lord never fails, so never fail to acknowledge and celebrate His perfect record of keeping His promises to His people.

NOTHING ESCAPES GOD'S NOTICE

Mordecai found out about the plot and told Queen Esther,
who in turn reported it to the king, giving credit to Mordecai.

ESTHER 2:22 NIV

Two men hatched an assassination plot against the king. One man overheard the treachery and got word to the king. Mordecai did the right thing when he spoke up, and the king would one day repay the kindness.

There will be times when doing the right thing doesn't seem to be appreciated. Sometimes it won't be noticed. Often it seems no one recognizes what you did. That happens to God all the time. Just remember that nothing escapes His notice. He knew you before you were born, and He knows about those acts of kindness, compassion, or obedience others tend to overlook.

Ask yourself, "Do I need the acknowledgment of others, or am I content if only God notices what I do?" One approach leads to discontent and the other to freedom. Choose wisely.

WAITING ON GOD, OUR HIGHEST JOY

Blessed art thou, O Lord: teach me thy statutes.

PSALM 119:12 KJV

As simple as it is, to one who has eyes, to walk all the day in the light of the sun, so simple and delightful can it become to a soul practiced in waiting on God, to walk all the day in the enjoyment of God's light and leading. What is needed to help us to such a life is just one thing: the real knowledge and faith of God as the one only source of wisdom and goodness, as ever ready and longing much to be to us all that we can possibly require—yes! This is the one thing we need.

If we but saw our God in His love, if we but believed that He waits to be gracious, that He waits to be our life and to work all in us—how this waiting on God would become our highest joy, the natural and spontaneous response of our hearts to His great love and glory!

GOD LOVES UNITY

"Go, gather together all the Jews who are in Susa, and have them all go without food so they can pray better for me."

ESTHER 4:16 NLV

God has always wanted unity for His family, and one of the primary evidences of unity among God's people is that they pray for one another. In Esther 4, the king signed a law that could have led to the genocide of God's people. The queen was part of that family. The new law meant she could be killed. This left many sad and worried.

For Queen Esther, the news led to a hard decision. She knew that going to talk to the king without being summoned could lead to her death. Knowing she faced a potential of two death sentences, Esther asked her people to be unified in fasting and prayer. This kind of prayer gave Esther the courage to start a conversation with the king that saved the lives of the Jews.

Unity might mean caring enough about something to pray—together.

A DETAIL-ORIENTED GOD

"Build a large boat from cypress wood and waterproof it with tar, inside and out. Then construct decks and stalls throughout its interior. Make the boat 450 feet long, 75 feet wide, and 45 feet high. Leave an 18-inch opening below the roof all the way around the boat. Put the door on the side, and build three decks inside the boat—lower, middle, and upper."

GENESIS 6:14–16 NLT

Noah's ark was a big boat. It had to be if it was to succeed in ferrying two of every kind of animal—and seven pairs of specific kinds—from a preflood world to a postflood world. But God didn't just give Noah a reason to build an ark. God gave Noah a detailed plan.

God isn't a distant deity, unconcerned about the problems in your life. He's present in the details and has a plan for you. It may not be as clear as the blueprints for an ark, but trusting Him will see you safely through each calamity that floods your life.

CLASSICS: CHARLES H. SPURGEON

BE LIKE JOSEPH. . .LIKE JESUS

And Joseph said unto his brethren, Come near to me, I pray you. And they came near. And he said, I am Joseph your brother, whom ye sold into Egypt.

GENESIS 45:4 KJV

Joseph is a very eminent type of Christ. When he was hated of his brethren because he protested against their sins and when they sold him for twenty pieces of silver, he was doubtless a portrait of the despised and rejected of men whom His disciple betrayed. Afterwards in his temptations in the house of Potiphar, in the slander and consequent imprisonment in the round house of Pharaoh's prison, in his after advancement, till he became lord over all the land of Egypt, we clearly see our blessed Lord right well portrayed. Indeed, so well is the picture drawn that there is scarcely a stroke even though it should seem to be a mere accidental incident of the picture which has not its symbolic meaning. You shall read the history of Joseph through twenty times, and yet you shall not have exhausted the type; you shall begin again and find still some fresh likeness between this despised son of Rachel and the Son of Mary who is also God over all, blessed for ever. Amen.

HOLY SPIRIT POWER

"You will receive power when the Holy Spirit comes on you; and you will be my witnesses in Jerusalem, and in all Judea and Samaria, and to the ends of the earth."

ACTS 1:8 NIV

A book entitled *Power Minutes for Men* would not be complete without an acknowledgment of the Christian's power source: God's Holy Spirit.

In Old Testament times, God's Spirit would "come upon" particular individuals, empowering them for particular service. This happened to judges like Gideon and Samson, kings such as Saul and David, and prophets like Ezekiel. But after Jesus' death and resurrection, He met with His followers and promised that they would receive the Spirit, a momentous event that happened on the following day of Pentecost.

Suddenly, Christians were speaking in other languages, boldly facing down hostile authorities, carrying the good news of Jesus throughout the known world. They were demonstrating the power that Jesus had promised. . .the power we as believers share in today.

GOD'S KIND OF MERCY

*"For I desire mercy, not sacrifice, and acknowledgment
of God rather than burnt offerings."*

HOSEA 6:6 NIV

We live in an increasingly angry, judgmental world.
But how many of us know what it means to be
hated? The writer of the Gospel of Matthew was a tax
collector—and in Matthew's day, everyone hated tax
collectors. Religious leaders and teachers viewed
tax collectors as thieves and sinners.

But Jesus saw things differently.

One day, while Jesus was having dinner at Matthew's
house, many tax collectors and sinners came and ate
with Him and His disciples. When the religious leaders
saw this, they asked His disciples, "Why does your
teacher eat with tax collectors and sinners?" On hearing this, Jesus said, "It is not the healthy who need a
doctor, but the sick. But go and learn what this means:
'I desire mercy, not sacrifice.' For I have not come to
call the righteous, but sinners" (Matthew 9:11–13 NIV).

Jesus was willing to forgive and then embrace the
worst in everyone. Shouldn't we be willing to extend
that kind of mercy to others?

THE PERFECT SAVIOR

What doth the LORD require of thee, but to do justly, and to love mercy, and to walk humbly with thy God?

MICAH 6:8 KJV

Viewed through the lens of the Old Testament Law, Jesus' suffering proves God's sense of justice and His vengeance against sin. Seen through the lens of the New Testament, Jesus' willingness to bear our punishment illustrates His own humility and the love of God.

When God commanded the Israelites to "do justly, and to love mercy, and to walk humbly" with Him, He provided a precise model of the perfection that Jesus would one day embody.

Our human ability to balance these three virtues is deeply lacking. But just mastering one of them is not enough—the Lord requires all of them. Thankfully, Jesus' sacrifice was complete—it ensures that as long as we keep striving toward the Father's standard, the Son's perfection will become our own.

GOD ALLOWS TROUBLE AND SUFFERING

He feared God and stayed away from evil.

JOB 1:1 NLT

Sometimes you can believe something that isn't necessarily true—at least not universally so. Job was of the opinion that if he stayed away from evil, God would bless him and keep trouble from approaching his doorstep. But trouble knocked, and this obedient man was left to wonder why.

Job's friends showed up and stated things that weren't true. They wanted Job to know that God rewards the obedient and punishes the wicked. They believed that when people struggle, it's because God has found a deficit in their lives.

This was not true in Job's case. He was obedient but tested. He was honest but suffered. He was committed but struggled. His losses were incredible, his health was in decline, and his friends were unsupportive.

The truth is that God sometimes allows trials and testing. Even Jesus promised trouble in this life.

God was with Job, and He saw the struggle long before it arrived. In Job's monumental battle, God had already overcome—and He had the answers Job would need.

CLASSICS: ANDREW MURRAY

GIVE UP EVERYTHING FOR CHRIST

And it came to pass in those days, when Moses was grown, that he went out unto his brethren, and looked on their burdens.

EXODUS 2:11 KJV

How wonderful is the place Moses occupies in the kingdom of God. A pattern of Jesus as a prophet, as a mediator, as an intercessor, in his meekness and his faithfulness, there are few of God's servants that stand higher. And what fitted him to take this place? Just this—the choice to give up everything for the reproach of Christ. Christian, wouldst thou live in the favor of God and enter into His tent to meet Him as Moses did? Wouldst thou be an instrument and a power of blessing, a man strong in faith? Seek to be perfectly separate from the spirit of the world, refuse its pleasure and honor and riches; count the contempt of God's people and the reproach of Christ thy treasures. Ask for the enlightening of the Holy Spirit to teach thee what true conformity to Christ is, in thy relation to the world, its culture, its possessions, its friendship. Beware of judging of what is lawful by any human standard: Christ alone can teach thee what it means to forsake all. . .and follow Him.

GOD KNOWS WHY

Job did not sin by charging God with wrongdoing.

JOB 1:22 NIV

The preliminary evidence was in, and all indications suggested God was unfair—and that Job wasn't as righteous as most thought. Neither conclusion was correct, and there was evidence yet to be discovered. Jumping to conclusions was easy but not helpful or productive.

Though Job could not understand why he was suffering, he still knew that God was good. This man loved God and served Him well, and he determined that he could not blame God for what he couldn't understand.

God does not always explain everything that happens in your life, but He promises to be with you in those things you don't understand. He is with you when others think they have a complete picture of your struggle. This God sees the end of your struggle and knows there's a better day coming. Don't resort to thinking Him cruel when you have yet to see the beauty from your personal ash pile.

A PLACE OF SECURITY

Then they said, "Come, let us build ourselves a city, with a tower that reaches to the heavens, so that we may make a name for ourselves; otherwise we will be scattered over the face of the whole earth."

GENESIS 11:4 NIV

After the flood, God gave out some simple instructions: "As for you, be fruitful and increase in number; multiply on the earth and increase upon it" (Genesis 9:7 NIV).

Instead of spreading over the earth as God intended, the people built a city. They wanted to provide their own security and make a name for themselves. But both of those goals belong to God's domain. As a result, God confused their language, causing them to spread out as originally intended.

When you are tempted to put security in your finances or garner praise for your accomplishments, you are building your own doomed tower. Put your tools away, find your security in God, and give Him the praise He alone deserves!

CLASSICS: CHARLES H. SPURGEON

GOD IS PACIFIED TOWARD YOU

And I will establish my covenant with thee; and thou shalt know that I am the LORD: that thou mayest remember, and be confounded, and never open thy mouth any more because of thy shame, when I am pacified toward thee for all that thou hast done, saith the Lord God.

EZEKIEL 16:62–63 KJV

O believer, God is pacified towards you, for your sin is covered; it is put away, all of it, and altogether. Since you have believed in Jesus Christ your sin has not become dimly visible, neither by searching may it be seen as a shadow in the distance; but God seeth it no more forever. . . .

And you may say, "O God, I will praise thee, for though thou wast angry with me, thine anger is turned away, and thou comfortest me." The many, the count-less hosts of sin that you have committed since your childhood are all scattered as a cloud, and the one black sin, which cost you more regret than many scores of others, has been removed as a thick cloud.

ETERNAL REWARDS

Be on your guard; stand firm in the faith;
be courageous; be strong.

1 CORINTHIANS 16:13 NIV

We can never think enough about God's sovereignty (His majesty and greatness), providence (His purposeful guidance and good provision), holiness (His absolute purity and amazing glory), love (His graciousness and merciful kindness), and mystery ("God alone knows"). Yes, we can rattle off a lot of other theological and biblical terms, but these are delightfully immense reminders of who God is.

When we think enough about who God really is, our response is humility and worship, awe and trust, dedication and praise, thankfulness and love. In turn, humility and worship, thankfulness, and love move us to think even more about God. And, we may note, to grow deeper and even more fruitful.

By enduring trials, resisting temptation, and never losing hope in God's eternal rewards, we will grow spiritually, persevere, endure to the end, and leave a good and godly legacy for generations to come. It's the life we all want to live, isn't it?

NOTHING DERAILS GOD'S PLAN

Then Job answered the Lord, and said, "I know that You can do all things. Nothing can put a stop to Your plans."

JOB 42:1–2 NLV

Job was nearing the end of a very long test. He'd asked questions for clarification, but for a long time, God the Instructor was silent. Job was left to consider his own questions and had only the input of other pupils who could give nothing better than textbook answers for his most critical questions.

Job did not curse God at any time, but he was weary of an exam he was certain he knew the answers to. And when God answered Job's arguments, it became very clear to him that God didn't need to explain His plan, a plan that would run its course and would not be derailed. In the end, the Instructor knew more than the student.

When you have more questions than answers, remember that your lack of understanding does not derail God's plan or diminish His wisdom.

THE GOD OF ALL COMFORT

Praise be to the God and Father of our Lord Jesus Christ, the Father of compassion and the God of all comfort, who comforts us in all our troubles, so that we can comfort those in any trouble with the comfort we ourselves receive from God.

2 CORINTHIANS 1:3–4 NIV

Roughly halfway through the book of 2 Corinthians, the apostle Paul wrote, "As servants of God we commend ourselves in every way: in great endurance; in troubles, hardships and distresses" (6:4 NIV). So when Paul refers to the Lord as "the God of all comfort" in today's scripture, he's speaking from personal experience.

You very probably haven't had to suffer for your faith the way Paul did, but that doesn't mean you won't face difficulties in your walk with Jesus. When you do, look past your own present situation and focus on the God who has promised to be your source of comfort, the God about whom the psalmist wrote, "My comfort in my suffering is this: Your promise preserves my life" (Psalm 119:50 NIV).

CLASSICS: CHARLES H. SPURGEON

GOD SHOULD RULE

And he said, I will make all my goodness pass before thee, and I will proclaim the name of the LORD before thee; and will be gracious to whom I will be gracious, and will shew mercy on whom I will shew mercy.

EXODUS 33:19 KJV

Because God is the maker, and creator, and sustainer of all things, He has a right to do as He wills with all His works. "Shall the thing formed say to him that formed it, Why hast thou made me thus? Hath not the potter power over the clay of the same lump to make one vessel unto honor, and another unto dishonor?" God's absolute supremacy and unlimited sovereignty naturally flow from His omnipotence, and if it were not so, the superlative excellence of the divine character would entitle Him to absolute dominion. He should be chief who is best. He who cannot err, being perfect in wisdom; He who will not err, being as perfect in holiness; He who can do no wrong, being supremely just; He who must act in accordance with the principles of kindness, seeing He is essentially love, is the most fitting person to rule.

THE LAW OF THE LORD

*His delight is in the law of the LORD; and in
his law doth he meditate day and night.*

PSALM 1:2 KJV

Do you find it strange to consider that some people think about God's law every day, both day and night? Here's why they do: those who really pay attention to God's law are delighted with what they find.

The law is, in simple terms, the way God wants people to live. Guys who "delight" in God's law understand that He lives by the very same rules. We can learn what God is like and what is most important to Him by looking at His example.

God knows that we help ourselves when we follow His law and hurt ourselves when we don't. He never asks us to do something that He doesn't do Himself—things like loving, forgiving, and showing mercy. Far from limiting our lives, God's law is all about our flourishing.

A GOD WHO HUMBLES

Though thou exalt thyself as the eagle, and though thou set thy nest among the stars, thence will I bring thee down, saith the Lord.

OBADIAH 4 KJV

Eagles are one of God's most breathtaking creations. President John F. Kennedy once wrote, "The fierce beauty and proud independence of this great bird aptly symbolizes the strength and freedom of America."

For many men, strength, pride, and independence are defining virtues. But when we embrace and then pursue those characteristics instead of humbling ourselves and putting Christ first in all things, we'll find ourselves moving farther and farther away from the Lord.

We should always remember that pride is deeply ingrained in our fallen human nature. That is why we should seek humility, knowing that God can humble us whenever or however He wants.

GOD SEES THE BIG PICTURE

And people from all around came to Egypt to buy grain from Joseph because the famine was severe throughout the world.

GENESIS 41:57 NLT

On the one hand, Joseph had a cool coat. On the other hand, he was nearly killed by his brothers, then sold into slavery and falsely accused of a crime that landed him in jail. For years, he was forgotten.

If Joseph's story had ended with him in jail, he probably wouldn't have thought that coat was worth the hassle. But God had a bigger job for Joseph than wearing some cool fashions. He needed to live through trials and tribulations to become Pharaoh's right-hand man. Why? So he could save the region from famine.

When you experience trials of your own, God may be preparing you for a special task down the road. God's vision is both clearer and longer than yours. Trust Him with your story, as Joseph did, and you'll end up saving more than you sacrificed.

CLASSICS: MATTHEW HENRY

JESUS CARRIES OUR SIN AWAY

And Aaron shall lay both his hands upon the head of the live goat, and confess over him all the iniquities of the children of Israel, and all their transgressions in all their sins, putting them upon the head of the goat, and shall send him away by the hand of a fit man into the wilderness: and the goat shall bear upon him all their iniquities unto a land not inhabited: and he shall let go the goat in the wilderness.

LEVITICUS 16:21–22 KJV

As Christ is the High Priest, so He is the sacrifice with which atonement is made; for He is all in all in our reconciliation to God. Thus He was figured by the two goats. The slain goat was a type of Christ dying for our sins; the scapegoat a type of Christ rising again for our justification. The atonement is said to be completed by putting the sins of Israel upon the head of the goat, which was sent away into a wilderness, a land not inhabited; and the sending away of the goat represented the free and full remission of their sins. He shall bear upon him all their iniquities. Thus Christ, the Lamb of God, takes away the sin of the world, by taking it upon Himself.

A LISTENING GOD

*Listen to my voice in the morning, LORD. Each morning
I bring my requests to you and wait expectantly.*

PSALM 5:3 NLT

Praying to a God you can't see may feel strange, but think about this: you can leave someone a voicemail and have complete faith that the other person will receive your message. Prayer is kind of like that, but there is no dclay—God hears immediately.

You will pray more when you remember that God always listens. You can know that prayer is never a wasted effort. Grab hold of the truth that your prayer provides direct access to the God who *wants* to hear from you.

It may seem like a one-sided conversation, but the truth of prayer is much better than that. When you pray, God listens. When you're done praying, open the Bible. That's when *you* take time to listen. Read each word with great expectation, and let God speak to you.

WHAT GOD SAYS HE WILL DO

*For all of God's promises have been fulfilled in Christ
with a resounding "Yes!" And through Christ, our "Amen"
(which means "Yes") ascends to God for his glory.*

2 CORINTHIANS 1:20 NLT

The need of your heart today may be weighing heavily on you. You may be single, married, separated, divorced, or widowed. You may be a young adult, closer to middle age, or a seasoned citizen. You may be in good health or bad. You may be rich or poor. Whatever your situation or stage, the circumstances and pressures of life may feel like they're beginning to crush you. Still. . .

Any of God's promises that we can claim in Jesus' name—that is, any promises God has made to us and millions of other Christians as His adopted children—are guaranteed. They will be fulfilled for us by God for His own glory.

What is the need of your heart today? God, in His grace, has promised to meet that need. Simply take Him at His Word. What He says He will do.

JESUS' INDESTRUCTIBLE LIFE

And what we have said is even more clear if another priest like Melchizedek appears, one who has become a priest not on the basis of a regulation as to his ancestry but on the basis of the power of an indestructible life.

HEBREWS 7:15–16 NIV

In the story of Abraham, a mysterious character named Melchizedek appears. This "king of Salem" and "priest of God Most High" (Genesis 14:18 NIV) accepted a tithe of the spoil Abraham had gained in a military engagement. Melchizedek is mentioned only one other time in the Old Testament, in Psalm 110:4 (NIV): "The LORD has sworn and will not change his mind: 'You are a priest forever, in the order of Melchizedek.' "

That was a messianic psalm from David, explained centuries later by the unnamed writer of Hebrews. He described Melchizedek as "without father or mother, without genealogy, without beginning of days or end of life" (Hebrews 7:3 NIV). Then Hebrews identifies Jesus as this "priest forever," based on "the power of an indestructible life" (verse 16 NIV).

Through His resurrection, Jesus demolished death. He will never die again. And when we believe in Him, He gives us His same indestructible life.

CLASSICS: D. L. MOODY

YOUR SINS ARE NOT REMEMBERED

And their sins and iniquities will I remember no more.

HEBREWS 10:17 KJV

We read: "Their sins and iniquities will I remember no more." Then when you turn to the eleventh chapter of the Hebrews and read God's roll of honor, you find that not one of the sins of any of those men of faith is mentioned. Abraham is spoken of as the man of faith; but it is not told how he denied his wife down in Egypt; all that had been forgiven. Moses was kept out of the Promised Land because he lost patience; but this is not mentioned in the New Testament, though his name appears in the apostle's roll of honor. Samson too is named, but his sins are not brought up again. Why, we even read of "righteous Lot"; he did not look much like a righteous man in the Old Testament story, but he has been forgiven, and God has made him "righteous."

If we are once forgiven by God, our sins will be remembered against us no more. This is God's eternal decree.

THE UNCHANGING GOD

*I am the LORD, I change not; therefore ye
sons of Jacob are not consumed.*

MALACHI 3:6 KJV

We live in a confusing world where nothing, not even life itself, is guaranteed a tomorrow. Amid all the uncertainty, it's easy to become cynical. After all, what is the purpose of *anything* if it will just eventually slip away like sand through our fingers?

What gives our lives meaning? The Bible supplies the answer: God.

The book of Ecclesiastes grapples deeply with the question of life's meaning. The author, after testing a variety of lifestyles and attitudes, eventually comes to the conclusion, "Fear God, and keep his commandments: for this is the whole duty of man" (12:13 KJV). Fads and opinions come and go, but our God—and His love for His children—remains steady.

He is the answer to all of this life's uncertainty.

CREATION TELLS OF GOD'S GREATNESS

The heavens are telling of the greatness of God and the great open spaces above show the work of His hands.

PSALM 19:1 NLV

Some people are blessed to live in a place where they can see the northern lights. Some enjoy a night sky that's dark enough to allow them to recognize constellations. The heavenly bodies all call down to you, seeking to bring applause to the God who made them.

There is a purpose for everything God created. "The work of His hands" may bring light to your day or brilliance to your night. God expressed Himself artistically when He created everything. He made all this divine art for you to enjoy. And beyond enjoyment, it should cause you to think about the God who still manages the details of this impressive creation.

God is great. His greatness shows through His Word, the lives He's changed, and the awesome creation that surrounds us.

A GOD WHO FORGETS

Do not remember the sins of my youth and my rebellious ways; according to your love remember me, for you, Lord, are good.

PSALM 25:7 NIV

You are aware of your past, and it's easy to dwell on every wrong choice you've made. The devil loves reminding us of a past filled with regret and lost time. But God? He's the only One who can truly—and willfully—forget your past. He does that when He forgives your sin. Once He forgives you, He never revisits your past or condemns you for it.

When the writer of Psalm 25 asked God not to remember his past sin, he recognized that it's God's love that keeps past sins forgotten and old lives buried. Forgiveness is refusing to bring up the past to hold it against another person. That is exactly what God does—perfectly.

CLASSICS: D. L. MOODY

NO BETTER LEADER THAN GOD

And they will tell it to the inhabitants of this land: for they have heard that thou Lord art among this people, that thou Lord art seen face to face, and that thy cloud standeth over them, and that thou goest before them, by day time in a pillar of a cloud, and in a pillar of fire by night.

NUMBERS 14:14 KJV

All that the children of Israel had to do in the wilderness was to follow the cloud. If the cloud rested, they rested; if the cloud moved forward, then they moved as it did. I can imagine the first thing Moses, or any of the people, did, when the grey dawn of morning broke, was to look up and see if the cloud was still over the camp. By night it was a pillar of fire, lighting up the camp and filling them with a sense of God's protecting care; by day it was a cloud shielding them from the fierce heat of the sun's rays and sheltering them from the sight of their enemies. Israel's Shepherd could lead His people through the pathless desert. Why? Because He made it. He knew every grain of sand in it. They could not have had a better leader through the wilderness than its Creator.

GOD THE SHEPHERD

Then he blessed Joseph and said, "May the God before whom my grandfather Abraham and my father, Isaac, walked—the God who has been my shepherd all my life, to this very day, the Angel who has redeemed me from all harm—may he bless these boys. May they preserve my name and the names of Abraham and Isaac. And may their descendants multiply greatly throughout the earth."

GENESIS 48:15–16 NLT

Jacob, also known as Israel, grew up in a shepherding family. His grandfather, Abraham, was a shepherd. His father, Isaac, was a shepherd. And Jacob worked for years with Laban's flocks to pay the bride price for first Leah then Rachel.

Jacob could see the similarities between God and shepherds and humanity and sheep. It isn't surprising then that on his deathbed, Jacob draws on the metaphor in blessing Joseph's children.

When God is your shepherd, you follow His lead, come at His call, and turn to Him when in danger. Living any other way is as foolish for a person as it is for a sheep.

NO ONE CAN FIGHT AGAINST GOD

"The day of the LORD is near for all nations. As you have done, it will be done to you; your deeds will return upon your own head."

OBADIAH 15 NIV

The prophet Obadiah wrote of God's judgment against Edom for its violence against the people of Israel. The Edomites lived in a rocky mountain range south of the Dead Sea. Edom's capital is known to us today as Petra, a stronghold carved into red sandstone cliffs overlooking the fertile valley of Arabah. The fortress seemed to them an unassailable monument to their savage might.

But, as we can see throughout the Bible, only God is all-powerful. No one can go against Him—or His people—and have any hope of victory. Obadiah's message was short and to the point: Edom would be stubble.

When it seems that your troubles and opposition are too much for you to handle, turn to the God who has never lost a single battle, let alone a war.

STRONG HOPE IN THE LORD

Be strong. Be strong in heart, all you who hope in the Lord.

PSALM 31:24 NLV

When circumstances make it impossible to even think about coping—be strong. When trouble works overtime to bring you down—be strong. When the struggle is greater than your patience—be strong.

The hope God wants you to have in Him is more than "giving it a shot." Our Christian hope is assurance fueled by faith. It's trust in the God you follow. It's the expectation that God will do what He promised.

Hope is not a wish but a steadfast confidence in a God who is more than able to handle the prayers of everyone who has ever lived on planet Earth.

So when you're living through your worst moments in life, stand, be strong, and always remember that Jesus loves you. Your strength is God's gift, your hope is in His love, and your heart is His home.

CLASSICS: CHARLES H. SPURGEON

LOOK TO THE LORD ALONE

And Hannah prayed, and said, My heart rejoiceth in the Lord,
mine horn is exalted in the Lord: my mouth is enlarged
over mine enemies; because I rejoice in thy salvation.

1 SAMUEL 2:1 KJV

It is very beautiful to see how the saints of old time were accustomed to find comfort in their God. When they came into sore straits, when troubles multiplied, when helpers failed, when earthly comforts were removed, they were accustomed to look to the Lord and to the Lord alone. Thus Hannah thinks of the Lord and comforts herself in His name.

By this means they were made strong and glad: they began to sing instead of sighing, and to work wonders instead of fainting under their burdens, even as here the inspired poetess sings, "My heart rejoiceth in the Lord, mine horn is exalted in the Lord." To them God was a reality, a present reality, and they looked to Him as their rock of refuge, their helper and defense, a very present help in time of trouble.

Can we not at the outset learn a valuable lesson from their example?

THE FACE OF JESUS CHRIST

For God, who said, "Let there be light in the darkness," has made this light shine in our hearts so we could know the glory of God that is seen in the face of Jesus Christ.

2 CORINTHIANS 4:6 NLT

That last phrase in today's scripture, "in the face of Jesus Christ," recalls a portrait painted by Rembrandt or one of his very gifted protégés. Sadly, the portrait is not on exhibit at the Metropolitan Museum of Art. It's one of the best depictions of Jesus Christ to come out of that era. His eyes are brown. His robe isn't white. His hair is anything but perfect. Most importantly, He looks like the real man He was—and is.

How good that God's unique Son, Jesus Christ, is loved by the Father, the Holy Spirit, the good angels, and all others who truly know Him. How good that we will see the glory of God in His wonderful face.

If we know and love Jesus as He really is, we are blessed men, indeed!

A GIFT YOU GIVE GOD

All the animals of the forest are mine,
and I own the cattle on a thousand hills.

PSALM 50:10 NLT

What could you possibly give God that He doesn't already have? He made the world, so all the land is His. He made the skies, so the clouds are His. He owns cattle, sheep, and everything in the sea. Taking from what He originally gave you to return to Him might seem like regifting, but that's exactly what He wants us to do—offer back to Him what He gave first. This shows that you honor His giving and trust Him to take care of you.

The one gift God really wants is fully within your control—He will never take it without your permission. That gift would be your heart—the core of who you are. It is a gift He longs for, but it's yours alone to give.

When you offer that gift, God responds with forgiveness and real life.

GOD KNOWS WHEN YOU'RE HURTING

Record my misery; list my tears on your scroll—are they not in your record?

PSALM 56:8 NIV

Never let anyone convince you that God doesn't care about your sorrow or is indifferent to your pain. The writer of Psalm 56 paints an incredible word picture of a God who keeps something much more personal than a scrapbook—namely, an account of your misery moments, tear times, and regret records.

God is not just an overseer. He doesn't simply assign a case worker to manage your affairs and provide Him with an overview at the next quarterly meeting. No—God Himself intervenes on your behalf, taking note of every moment of despair, depression, and despondency you experience.

When grief reaches escape velocity, God knows. He is near when hearts are breaking and compassion is most needed. Is it any wonder He's called good?

CLASSICS: ANDREW MURRAY

THE LORD HIMSELF FIGHTS FOR YOU

The Lord your God which goeth before you, he shall fight for you, according to all that he did for you in Egypt before your eyes.

DEUTERONOMY 1:30 KJV

The Holy Spirit will seal our faith with a divine experience; we shall see the glory of God. But this is His work: ours is, when all appears dark and cold, in the face of all that nature or experience testifies, still each moment to believe in Jesus as our all-sufficient sanctification, in whom we are perfected before God. Complaints as to want of feeling, as to weakness or deadness, seldom profit: it is the soul that refuses to occupy itself with itself, either with its own weakness or the strength of the enemy, but only looks to what Jesus is and has promised to do, to whom progress in holiness will be a joyful march from victory to victory. "The Lord Himself doth fight for you"; this thought, so often repeated in connection with Israel's possession of the promised land, is the food of faith: in conscious weakness, in presence of mighty enemies, it sings the conqueror's song.

THE GOD WHO IS

*And God said to Moses, "I AM WHO I AM." And He said,
"Say to the Israelites, 'I AM has sent me to you.'"*

EXODUS 3:14 NLV

Names are important. Bible characters often lived into the roles promised by their names. Joshua's name means "YAHWEH is salvation," and he led Israel into the promised land. God famously changed Abram's name (which means "multitude") to Abraham (which means "father of many"), and his offspring fathered multiple nations.

But the most important name in the Bible is God's own: I AM.

We serve the God who *is*. He is eternal, existing from before time began and into the never-ending future. He is the same God who commissioned Moses to rescue the Israelites from Egypt, who sent His Son to die on the cross, and who is coming back for us!

Whatever your name happens to be, the eternal God calls you His own.

NOTHING BETTER THAN GOD'S LOVE

Because your love is better than life, my lips will glorify you.

PSALM 63:3 NIV

God has loved, will always love, and is love. All of love's unselfish acts of kindness came from God's heart to mankind. It is His love that convinces sinners to accept His gift of rescue. It is His love that invites people to follow His example. It is His love that breaks down walls of pride that make you believe you don't need God.

This love from a good God is to be preferred to life itself. It's better than your best moment and continues after your last breath. So let His goodness seep into your heart to find an honorable response that others can see and hear.

Nothing can come between you and God's love. Run away from God and He will follow. Tell Him you don't need Him and He will still love you. Chase sin and He will still call your name and invite you back home.

God's love is always better than the life you leave behind.

GOD'S PROMISE OF REWARD

We do not give up. Our human body is wearing out.
But our spirits are getting stronger every day.

2 CORINTHIANS 4:16 NLV

This vital challenge echoes throughout the rest of the New Testament. This includes Galatians 6:9 (KJV): "Let us not be weary in well doing: for in due season we shall reap, if we faint not," and 2 Thessalonians 3:13 (NIV): "Never tire of doing what is good."

This also includes Hebrews 10:35–36 ("Do not throw away your trust, for your reward will be great. You must be willing to wait without giving up," and Hebrews 12:3 (KJV): "Consider him that endured such contradiction of sinners against himself, lest ye be wearied and faint in your minds."

Bottom line: trust the Lord fully, always. Keep doing God's will no matter what. Never forget what Jesus Christ deeply suffered for you. Remember your promised rewards to be enjoyed eternally.

CLASSICS: ANDREW MURRAY

COME TO GOD AS A CHILD

Whosoever therefore shall humble himself as this little child, the same is greatest in the kingdom of heaven. And whoso shall receive one such little child in my name receiveth me.

MATTHEW 18:4–5 KJV

The disciples had come to Jesus with the question, "Who is the greatest in the kingdom of heaven?" He spoke so often of the kingdom; to them it suggested the idea of power and glory; they could not but wonder who would have the highest place. How utterly strange and incomprehensible must have been the answer Jesus gave to their question. He called a little child and set him in the midst of them. He told them that as long as they were thinking of who would be greatest, they could not even enter the kingdom; they must first become as little children: and then in the kingdom the humblest and the most childlike would be the highest. And whoever should receive one such little child in Jesus' name, should receive Himself. The deeper the sympathy with the child-nature, recognizing Jesus and His name in it, the closer and more complete the union with Himself.

POWER, EVEN FOR THE UNDESERVING

Samson prayed to the Lord, "Sovereign Lord, remember me. Please, God, strengthen me just once more, and let me with one blow get revenge on the Philistines for my two eyes."

JUDGES 16:28 NIV

Yes, God is powerful. Yes, He shares that power with His faithful followers. But what happens when we've failed, when *faithful* isn't the best word to describe us?

For an answer, we turn to the story of Samson. The strongman judge of Israel was set apart for God's work even before he was born. Then he followed the Nazirite vow imposed upon him by allowing his hair to grow and grow. A terribly undisciplined man, Samson had plenty of sketchy moments but somehow still protected God's people from their enemies.

Until Delilah, that is—even many non-Christians recognize her name as Samson's downfall. Less familiar may be the disgraced judge's final prayer: "Please, God, strengthen me just once more, and let me with one blow get revenge on the Philistines."

God said yes. He is gracious even when we've sinned. But far better to follow His rules all along.

GOD MOVES AS HE SEES FIT

*He got down on his knees and prayed, giving thanks
to his God, just as he had done before.*

DANIEL 6:10 NIV

The Bible tells us that Daniel so distinguished himself among the governors and administrators of his day that the king planned to set him over the entire kingdom. Upon hearing this news, his fellow governors and administrators tried to find grounds for charges against him.

But God had a plan for Daniel's deliverance.

There will be times when we are treated unjustly, even treacherously. Everything inside us will want to fight back. But like Daniel, we must be willing to go against the flow, trust God, and let Him move as He sees fit, when He sees fit.

Daniel's peers turned his faith into a felony. Daniel turned that felony into continued prayer. The men who maliciously accused Daniel were cast into the lions' den. And Daniel prospered during the reign of Darius the king—only because He trusted God to move on his behalf.

INFINITE YET PERSONAL

His name shall be called Wonderful, Counsellor, The mighty God, The everlasting Father, The Prince of Peace.

ISAIAH 9:6 KJV

God is often depicted as a Being who sits far above the clouds, staring down at humanity with a blend of frustration and indifference. But the Bible's picture is much different.

Centuries before Jesus' birth, Isaiah was inspired to write a concise, eloquent depiction of the coming Savior. Today's scripture, often quoted around Christmastime, uses the words *wonderful*, *mighty*, and *everlasting* in conjunction with terms like *counsellor* and *peace*. This mixture of unthinkable strength and personal care can only be found in Jesus, God in human flesh.

Patient and loving enough to counsel the penitent soul yet strong enough to control the entire universe— that is the God we serve.

CLASSICS: D. L. MOODY

MAN'S WEAKNESS LEANING ON GOD'S STRENGTH

The eternal God is thy refuge, and underneath are the everlasting arms: and he shall thrust out the enemy from before thee; and shall say, Destroy them.

DEUTERONOMY 33:27 KJV

God can do what He has done before. He kept Joseph in Egypt; Moses before Pharaoh; Daniel in Babylon; and enabled Elijah to stand before Ahab in that dark day. And I am so thankful that these I have mentioned were men of like passions with ourselves. It was God who made them so great.

What man wants is to look to God. Real true faith is man's weakness leaning on God's strength. When man has no strength, if he leans on God, he becomes powerful. The trouble is that we have too much strength and confidence in ourselves.

CONFIDENCE IN GOD

I am always with You. You hold me by my right hand.

PSALM 73:23 NLV

The writer of Psalm 73 stated that he was always with God. The opposite side of the coin is even more true— God is always with you. There will be times when you feel alone, but loneliness is a false positive. It may seem real, but it never takes into account the vital truth that God won't leave you to suffer alone.

Children gain confidence from being in the presence of good parents. The same idea applies to being in God's presence. You can be absolutely confident in the fact that He leads, guides, and walks with you, so there's never a need to feel alone.

Take God's hand and trust His ability to lead. Then? Walk on.

GOD VS. OUR EXCUSES

Moses said to the Lord, "Pardon your servant, Lord. I have never been eloquent, neither in the past nor since you have spoken to your servant. I am slow of speech and tongue." The Lord said to him, "Who gave human beings their mouths? Who makes them deaf or mute? Who gives them sight or makes them blind? Is it not I, the Lord? Now go; I will help you speak and will teach you what to say."

EXODUS 4:10–12 NIV

When Moses was tasked with returning to Egypt, he was reluctant to go. Maybe because of his stutter. Or maybe he didn't feel like he belonged. After all, he was a Hebrew raised in Pharaoh's household, while his fellow Hebrews were slaves. But Moses wasn't returning to Egypt under his own authority. He was going to be God's representative.

God has tasked us to represent Him too. No matter how reluctant we might be, God can overcome our excuses and empower us with His words. We must simply be willing to go.

TIME WITH GOD

*A single day in your courts is better
than a thousand anywhere else!*

PSALM 84:10 NLT

Many of us have in mind a place we've always wanted to visit, but something—usually time or money—has prevented the trip. But let's say that you had the freedom to go anywhere in the world, all expenses paid. How exciting would that be? What kind of stories would you have in the years to come? Would it be the highlight of your life?

The writer of Psalm 84 didn't think so. He believed that one day with God was more satisfying than a thousand spent anywhere else. God provides friendship that can transform your life and offer contentment unmatched by the most impressive views, desirable destinations, and critically acclaimed events.

Enter God's presence for wisdom, life, and love. There is no better way to spend your time.

CLASSICS: ANDREW MURRAY

GOD'S QUICKENING POWER

And God said, Sarah thy wife shall bear thee a son indeed; and thou shalt call his name Isaac: and I will establish my covenant with him for an everlasting covenant, and with his seed after him. . . . But my covenant will I establish with Isaac, which Sarah shall bear unto thee at this set time in the next year.

GENESIS 17:19, 21 KJV

In the birth of Isaac, [Abraham] had learned to know God as the giver of life, even where he was as good as dead. He knew and trusted his God, as *God who quickeneth the dead and calleth the things that are not as though they were.* And what is it that will give our faith the same all-victorious strength and prepare us for the same mighty exhibition of God's quickening power on our behalf? If we are to have the same faith and the same experience of God, we must be prepared to make the same sacrifice. Our lesson. . .leads us to the very deepest roots of the life of faith. The deeper we are willing to enter into the death to self, the more shall we know of the mighty power of God and the perfect blessedness of a perfect trust.

A GOD WHO LEADS

*And the Lord went before them by day in a pillar of
a cloud, to lead them the way; and by night in a pillar
of fire, to give them light; to go by day and night.*

EXODUS 13:21 KJV

While Moses may have been the one to interact with
Pharaoh on behalf of the Israelites, he wasn't in charge.
God was. When the Israelites left Egypt, Moses may
have been at the head of the procession, but everyone
was following God.

In those days, God literally led the people as a pillar
of cloud by day and a pillar of fire by night. Do you
ever wish following God were that simple?

In some ways, it is. God may not show up in visible
ways today, but He's given us something even better:
His Word to explain things and His Spirit, living inside
us, to make it clear. God still leads His people. Are you
paying attention?

THE GOD WHO INSTRUCTS

Blessed is the one you discipline, LORD, the one you teach from your law; you grant them relief from days of trouble.

PSALM 94:12–13 NIV

What kind of rescue would God be providing if He didn't also give you new direction? How can God redeem if you have no intention of leaving your old lifestyle behind? That's like acknowledging that you need medical help but refusing to do what the doctor tells you to do.

It is true that you can come to God just as you are, but He knows you will gain no benefit without the transformation only He can provide. Your obedience is what leads to that transformation.

You should never refuse God's wisdom when He tells you something in your life needs to change. You may not enjoy His instruction, but you can be assured that following it will provide relief during troubled days ahead.

HOW GOD WORKS THROUGH YOU

I am crucified with Christ: nevertheless I live; yet not I, but Christ liveth in me: and the life which I now live in the flesh I live by the faith of the Son of God, who loved me, and gave himself for me.

GALATIANS 2:20 KJV

A mentor asked a younger friend, "Are you making a dent in the universe?" The friend winced. Dents are usually followed by disgruntled drivers, police reports, insurance agencies, repair shops, and bills. Then again, the mentor was trying to avoid the overused word *impact*. Perhaps "positive lasting fruit" or "results" are what we want to produce in this life. They're certainly what God wants to produce through us.

How? The secret is revealed in today's scripture. What has Jesus been doing inside you lately? Christ-centered spiritual disciplines are the spaces for Him to work in our lives. They include music, prayer, silence, Bible reading, meditation, going to church, conversation, giving, service, receiving correction, committed friendships, and seeing God at work in others and through His creation. What's your favorite?

CLASSICS: D. L MOODY

WELCOME IN GOD'S PRESENCE

And, behold, the veil of the temple was rent in twain from the top to the bottom; and the earth did quake, and the rocks rent.

MATTHEW 27:51 KJV

When Christ's work was done, the veil of the temple was rent from the top to the bottom. God came out of the holy of holies, and man can now go in. He makes all His people in this dispensation kings and priests. Everyone can come right into the presence of God Himself.

In the Jewish dispensation none but the high priest could enter into the holy of holies; but Christ's veil being rent, God came out and man can go in through the veil of His flesh. "Let us therefore draw near with a true heart, in full assurance of faith, having our hearts sprinkled from an evil conscience, and our bodies washed with pure water."

GOD WANTS YOU TO "SAY SO"

Let the redeemed of the Lord say so.

PSALM 107:2 KJV

God has made it clear that you mean something to Him, and He wants you to talk about what He means to you. His love for you began before you were born and will last long after your final breath. He's made it clear He wants to establish new life among old sinners—including you.

So if you've been rescued, redeemed, and transformed—say so. When God has been good to you—say so. When you're learning new wisdom—say so.

It's easy sometimes to hide your light and pretend you're no different from everyone else. But others are looking for the better life that you have. They may not know what they're looking for, and they may never know unless you—say so.

Say it alone or with others, but resist the urge to hide the truth of your redemption. God has done an eternity-altering thing, so talk about it. . .out loud.

A GOD WHO COMMUNICATES

"Praise be to the name of God for ever and ever; wisdom and power are his. He changes times and seasons; he deposes kings and raises up others. He gives wisdom to the wise and knowledge to the discerning."

DANIEL 2:20–21 NIV

As Daniel prepared to interpret the Babylonian king Nebuchadnezzar's bizarre and troubling dream, God communicated the dream's meaning in a vision. Daniel was so grateful that he spoke wonderful words of praise to the Lord for His wisdom and power. . .and for the amazing truth that God communicates with His people.

"He gives wisdom to the wise and knowledge to the discerning." In speaking these words, Daniel gave voice to his gratitude for the fact that the Lord isn't some distant, silent Creator but a loving God who *wants* to communicate with His people.

Our God still communicates with us today— through His written Word and through the Holy Spirit, who brings illumination to the lessons and wisdom He has given us in that Word. Our part in that arrangement is to seek and listen.

FORETASTES OF GOD'S HEAVENLY BLESSINGS

*Praise be to the God and Father of our Lord
Jesus Christ, who has blessed us in the heavenly
realms with every spiritual blessing in Christ.*

EPHESIANS 1:3 NIV

Two thousand years ago, Jesus Christ's earthly ministry gave the men and women, youth and children around Him amazing foretastes of what is eternal for each of His followers. Those foretastes cover a wide horizon. To name but a few: seeing individuals raised from the dead, seeing other persons healed spiritually, seeing still others healed physically, and seeing yet other persons healed psychologically.

Let's not make the mistake, however, of thinking that wonderful foretastes of heaven aren't ours to enjoy today. As a follower of Jesus Christ, our sins—past, present, and future—already are forgiven, yet we experience forgiveness anew each time we confess our sins. Immediately afterward, we should slow down and savor that specific experience of being forgiven. When we do, we get to enjoy a delicious preview of heaven. Taste and see.

CLASSICS: CHARLES H. SPURGEON

MARK THE HAND OF GOD

Then Samuel took a stone, and set it between
Mizpeh and Shen, and called the name of it Ebenezer,
saying, Hitherto hath the Lord helped us.

1 SAMUEL 7:12 KJV

It is certainly a very delightful thing to mark the hand of God in the lives of ancient saints. How profitable an occupation to observe God's goodness in delivering David out of the jaw of the lion and the paw of the bear; His mercy in passing by the transgression, iniquity and sin of Manasseh; His faithfulness in keeping the covenant made with Abraham; or His interposition on the behalf of the dying Hezekiah.

But, beloved, would it not be even more interesting and profitable for us to mark the hand of God in our own lives? Ought we not to look upon our own history as being at least as full of God, as full of His goodness and His truth, as much a proof of His faithfulness and veracity as the lives of any of the saints who have gone before? I think we do our Lord an injustice when we suppose that He wrought all His mighty acts in days of yore.

GOD'S ETERNAL WORD

Forever, O Lord, Your Word will never change in heaven.

PSALM 119:89 NLV

You can change your socks, your screen resolution, the oil in your car. You can change your hairstyle, your car, your home. You're used to change, right? Maybe that's why it seems strange to read that God does *not* change. Ever. His love does not change. His faithfulness is entirely changeless. And His Word does not change.

If you want to reinvent yourself in a lasting way, God invites you to start by getting to know the unchangeable Him. The only change you will make that is entirely good is when you accept God's offer to transform—or change—you. This is new life, and it looks a lot more like Him.

Rely on God's Word, rest in His care, hold tight to His promise to never abandon you. These things are all part of the God who never changes but promises to change you.

A PRAISEWORTHY GOD

The Lord is my strength and song. He is the One Who saves me. He is my God and I will praise Him. He is my father's God and I will honor Him.

EXODUS 15:2 NLV

After God delivered the Israelites from Pharaoh's clutches on the far shore of the Red Sea, Moses stopped to write a song. If you've ever had a song stuck in your head, you know how effectively songs can help you remember things.

Moses wanted all of Israel to listen and recall how God had delivered them from certain death. Moses recognized God as the source of His people's strength, as the song that provides melody and rhythm to life. Even today, God reveals Himself in power as worthy of all praise.

God's Red Sea rescue foreshadowed the ultimate salvation of His people: through Jesus' death on the cross. Moses expressed his praise through song. How will you praise God today?

GOD ENABLES YOUR WORK

You may say to yourself, "My power and the strength of my hands have produced this wealth for me." But remember the LORD your God, for it is he who gives you the ability to produce wealth.

DEUTERONOMY 8:17–18 NIV

A lot of guys take pride in their abilities and hard work—they make one-, five-, and ten-year plans and accomplish every goal by the sheer force of their will. Other guys can't even imagine that. Today's scripture can be a challenge to both types.

These words of Moses, spoken to the Israelites about to enter their promised land, remind the hard drivers that anything they accomplish still comes by way of God. "It is he who gives you the ability to produce wealth." For the other guys, Deuteronomy 8:17–18 may remove some of the pressure the world lays on them. Whatever they achieve is still a gift of God.

The key for all of us? "*Remember* the Lord your God." Whatever skills and personality He's given you, keep Him in your thoughts at all time. In God's economy, that is success.

CLASSICS: ANDREW MURRAY

A MAN GOD CAN TRUST AND USE

[God] raised up unto them David to be their king; to whom also he gave their testimony, and said, I have found David the son of Jesse, a man after mine own heart, which shall fulfil all my will.

ACTS 13:22 KJV

Of the two expressions God uses here of David, we often hear the former: "a man after Mine own heart." The use of the latter, "who shall do all My will," is much less frequent. And yet it is no less important than the other.

A man after Mine own heart: that speaks of the deep unseen mystery of the pleasure a man can give to God in heaven. *Who shall do all My will*: that deals with the life down here on earth which can be seen and judged by men. Let us seek and get full hold of the truth that it is *the man who does all God's will* who is the man after His own heart. Such men God seeks: when He finds them He rejoices over them with great joy: they are the very men He needs, men He can trust and use. His heart, with its hidden divine perfections, reveals itself in His will: he that seeks and loves *and does all His will* is a man altogether after His own heart: the man of absolute surrender to God's will.

THE SOUL-SCULPTOR

*But now, O Lord, thou art our father; we are the clay,
and thou our potter; and we all are the work of thy hand.*

ISAIAH 64:8 KJV

The Bible teaches that God is our Creator. . .and in more ways than one. The Lord molded Adam from the dust and breathed life into him, but ever since the Fall, God has engaged in creation of a different sort—an inward creation of renewed hearts.

"Create in me a clean heart, O God," the psalmist David begged after committing adultery with Bathsheba, "and renew a right spirit within me" (Psalm 51:10 KJV). This is the cry that should be on the lips of every human being—the plea for re-creation.

"If any man be in Christ, he is a new creature," the apostle Paul taught (2 Corinthians 5:17 KJV). This goes far beyond a new coat of paint or some other cosmetic improvement. When you allow Him to, God will completely re-create your life through Jesus Christ.

GOD PROVIDES LIGHT

I long for the Lord more than sentries long for the dawn.
PSALM 130:6 NLT

Imagine a soldier in wartime. He has been assigned night patrol. Every shadow could mean an enemy approaches. Every cracking twig could signal doom. His nerves are frayed as he anxiously waits for his patrol to end. This soldier's greatest prayer is for the dawning of a new day. Once the dark night ends, he will find a time of rest. In that light, he will finally be able to relax.

Longing for God is something like that. When you don't have God, you walk in darkness, fear the darkness, and worry because you have no idea what to do, how to do it, or where to go.

But following God is like a new morning after a dark night. What worried you most can't begin to stand up to Him, for darkness must run away from light.

Long for God. A new morning is arriving.

THE GOD OF PROVIDENCE

In him we were also chosen, having been predestined according to the plan of him who works out everything in conformity with the purpose of his will.

EPHESIANS 1:11 NIV

Did you know that the word *providence* (referring to the Lord) doesn't appear in a single Bible verse? In some ways, that's fitting. After all, "providence" speaks of God's eternal, infinite, and (mostly) invisible hand at work in nations, tribes, families, and individuals. It's God's purposeful guidance and good provision for each.

Heroes of faith—Abraham, Joseph, Ruth, Ezra, Esther, and many others—rejoiced in God's providence, which increased their faith and trust in Him. The Lord assured the prophet Isaiah: "I make known the end from the beginning, from ancient times, what is still to come. I say, 'My purpose will stand, and I will do all that I please'" (Isaiah 46:10 NIV).

So, does God's purposeful guidance and good provision permeate your life? Yes! Life is abundant when you recognize and rejoice in both today.

CLASSICS: CHARLES H. SPURGEON

BECAUSE HE IS GOD

Know ye that the LORD he is God: it is he that hath made us, and not we ourselves; we are his people, and the sheep of his pasture.

PSALM 100:3 KJV

Really to know the deity of God, to get some idea of what is meant by saying that He is God, is to have the very strongest argument forced upon one's soul for obedience and worship. The godhead gave authority to the first law that was ever promulgated when God forbade man to touch the fruit of a certain tree. Why might not Adam pluck the fruit? Simply and only because God forbade it. Had God permitted, it had been lawful; God's prohibition made it sin to eat thereof. God gave no reason for saying to Adam, "In the day thou eatest thereof thou shalt surely die." His commandment, seeing He was God, was the supremest reason, and to have questioned His right to make the law would have been in itself flat rebellion. God was to be obeyed simply because He was God. . . .

Because the Lord is God therefore should we serve Him with gladness and come before His presence with singing.

PRAISE GOD'S NAME!

Praise the LORD, for the LORD is good; sing praise to his name, for that is pleasant.

PSALM 135:3 NIV

Music is a gift from God. It's art in melody. It's beauty for the ear. It's pleasant to God, and He encourages it. Music moves the heart from gratitude to worship. It invites you to say the name of the One who rescued you and to celebrate the profound goodness of the rescuing God.

The Bible says that God Himself sings over His people because they bring Him joy. He encouraged people to play instruments and sing new songs in return.

Is it possible that God uses music as one more way to connect you to His heart? Could it be that a song demonstrates the stunning beauty of God's creation? What if music serves to encourage you to let God direct the world around you in a symphony that brings praise to your conversation and hope to your heart?

Sing praise to His wonderful name.

WORTHY OF HONOR

"You have set yourself up against the Lord of heaven. . . . You praised the gods of silver and gold, of bronze, iron, wood and stone, which cannot see or hear or understand. But you did not honor the God who holds in his hand your life and all your ways."

DANIEL 5:23 NIV

Daniel spoke a harsh message of rebuke to Belshazzar. The reason? Because the Persian king had not honored God. In fact, he worshipped worthless, inanimate statues instead of the one true God.

The Bible makes it abundantly clear that God is worthy and due one thing from us humans: honor as our all-holy, all-loving Creator and heavenly Father. That is not only our responsibility but our privilege as His beloved children.

When you honor God in your every word, thought, and deed, you draw yourself closer to Him in every way . . .you glorify Him and set an example those around you need to hear and see.

OUR WARRIOR GOD

"The Lord is a warrior; the Lord is his name."

EXODUS 15:3 NIV

When it comes to fighting for His chosen people, God never backs down. While the Bible says and shows that God is love, it also shows that God is a warrior. In fact, it is because of His love that He fights to protect those who bear His name.

Does that mean God will always grant victory to His followers? Yes, though that victory may not look like you expect. The God who divided the Red Sea and decimated Pharaoh's army is the same One who allowed Roman soldiers to take Jesus to the cross.

God's victories are grander than we can imagine. His strategies are further-seeing than our lifespans. His ability to make war on the enemy is unmatched.

Whatever fights you face today, rest assured that the Lord is a warrior who fights for you.

CLASSICS: MATTHEW HENRY

ENTITLED TO A BETTER PARADISE

As for Mephibosheth, said the king, he shall eat at my table, as one of the king's sons.

2 SAMUEL 9:11 KJV

Now because David was a type of Christ, his Lord and son, his root and offspring, let his kindness to Mephibosheth serve to illustrate the kindness and love of God our Savior toward fallen man, which yet he was under no obligation to, as David was to Jonathan.

Man was convicted of rebellion against God and, like Saul's house, under a sentence of rejection from Him, was not only brought low and impoverished, but lame and impotent, made so by the fall. The Son of God enquires after this degenerate race, that enquired not after Him, comes to seek and save them. To those of them that humble themselves before Him and commit themselves to Him, He restores the forfeited inheritance, He entitles them to a better paradise than that which Adam lost and takes them into communion with Himself, sets them with His children at His table and feasts them with the dainties of heaven.

Lord, what is man, that thou shouldst thus magnify him!

A MARVELOUS CREATOR

I will praise thee; for I am fearfully and wonderfully made: marvellous are thy works; and that my soul knoweth right well.

PSALM 139:14 KJV

God made you like no one else in history. You're as unique as any of the billions of other human beings who have ever lived. And that makes your Creator worthy of your worship.

You have seen God's goodness. You've recognized His wonder. Now? Worship. Then? Praise.

It can be easy to see God's amazing wonder in nature, but a little tougher to think of yourself as one of His marvelous creations. It can be easy to believe that God loves others but hard to comprehend His love for you.

When God created you He wanted to demonstrate His love. Now, He wants you to recognize how important you are to Him.

GOD ENJOYS OUR PRAYERS

I pray that the eyes of your heart may be enlightened in order that you may know. . .his incomparably great power for us who believe. That power is the same as the mighty strength he exerted when he raised Christ from the dead and seated him at his right hand in the heavenly realms.

EPHESIANS 1:18–20 NIV

Did you know God the Father unleashes His "incomparably great power" in answer to the prayers of Jesus Christ (Romans 8:34, Hebrews 7:25), the prayers of the Holy Spirit (Romans 8:26–27), and the prayers of His people?

For God, prayer is a multisensory experience. Our prayers are a sweet-smelling incense to Him. Our offerings of praise and thanksgiving taste like choice meats and aged wine. He hears our humble, earnest prayers and gladly answers them. He feels our struggles, sufferings, and griefs and cares for us. He sees the beginning and the end and richly blesses us each day.

A BETTER DIRECTION

*Do not let my heart turn to any sinful thing,
to do wrong with men who sin.*

PSALM 141:4 NLV

Men hate to fail. We work hard, play hard, and take it hard when we don't feel we measure up. Sound familiar?

Maybe that's why men tend to be competitive, why we feel the need to prove we're good at something— perhaps better than most. If we can prove this to ourselves, then maybe we're okay. But there will be times when our best efforts seem worthless. That's why we need to rethink the value of our friendship with God. He accepts us just as we are, but He has a plan for each of us, a plan that includes helping us to live and think in ways that please Him.

Because men are competitive, they often try to outdo each other in the category of sin. But God wants to move us in a better direction—one that rejects sin and accepts His help.

CLASSICS: D. L. MOODY

THE FATHER LOVES YOU STILL

I will arise and go to my father, and will say unto him, Father, I have sinned against heaven, and before thee, and am no more worthy to be called thy son: make me as one of thy hired servants. And he arose, and came to his father. But when he was yet a great way off, his father saw him, and had compassion, and ran, and fell on his neck, and kissed him.

LUKE 15:18–20 KJV

What brought the prodigal home? It was the thought that his father loved him. Suppose the news had reached him that he was cast off and that his father did not care for him anymore; would he have gone back? Never! But the thought dawned upon him that his father loved him still: so he rose up and went back to his home.

Dear reader, the love of the Father ought to bring us back to Him. It was Adam's calamity and sin that revealed God's love. When Adam fell God came down and dealt in mercy with him. If anyone is lost it will not be because God does not love him: it will be because he has resisted the love of God.

GOD THE TEACHER

For the Lord grants wisdom! From his mouth come knowledge and understanding. He grants a treasure of common sense to the honest. He is a shield to those who walk with integrity.

PROVERBS 2:6–7 NLT

Who is God? Well, He's a lot of things—all of them good. But in the verse above, He's identified as a teacher who gives His people a full-ride scholarship of wisdom. There's no tuition, but you're required to pay attention. He offers knowledge and common sense, but you'll need to listen, apply what He's taught, and believe what He says.

Be honest. Walk with integrity. Accept God's scholarship and improve life. It sounds easier than it is. Like any educational pursuit, following God and accepting His wisdom means accepting greater responsibility as you learn right from wrong, good from bad, and what God wants you to do. God teaches so you can learn to do what is right in His eyes.

GOD'S GIFT OF HOLINESS

"Who is like you among the gods, O Lord—glorious in holiness, awesome in splendor, performing great wonders?"

EXODUS 15:11 NLT

God stands alone. While people have found no end of things to worship—celebrities, politicians, athletes, business tycoons, wealth, beauty, self—God alone is worthy of our praise. He is perfect in every possible way, existing in and for His own glory.

Humanity, in its fallen state, strives for the glory that belongs to God alone. We worship lesser things and attempt to gain glory for ourselves, but God's holiness is unattainable by our efforts. That's why He's bestowed it on us as a gift.

God is holy. There is none like Him. But when He sent His Son to take away our sins, He gave us His holiness and welcomed us into His family. Now, we are as like Him as we can be, set apart for a special purpose, ready to praise Him as He deserves.

GOD'S PERFECT WISDOM

If you are wise, your wisdom is a help to you. If you laugh at the truth, you alone will suffer for it.

PROVERBS 9:12 NLV

Wisdom is the perfect guide. It walks with you at the start of your journey and delivers you to your intended destination. Wisdom is honorable, helpful, and sensible.

Perhaps this is nothing new to you, but perfect wisdom comes from God. He expressed Himself in the Bible, so the logical conclusion is God placed His wisdom in His Word. That wisdom is truth.

The truth you need is found in the Bible. God has given you everything you need to connect your choices to His wisdom. When you reject that truth, you become disconnected from wisdom. But when you accept it, you open yourself up to God's best for you.

CLASSICS: ANDREW MURRAY

GIVE GOD YOUR WHOLE HEART

Let your heart therefore be perfect with the Lord our God, to walk in his statutes, and to keep his commandments, as at this day.

1 KINGS 8:61 KJV

He is Almighty God: all things are possible to Him: He holds rule over all. All His power is working for those who trust Him. And all He asks of His servant is that he shall be perfect with Him: give Him his whole heart, his perfect confidence. God Almighty with all His power is wholly for thee; be thou wholly for God. The knowledge and faith of what God is lies at the root of what we are to be: "I am Almighty God: be thou perfect." As I know Him whose power fills heaven and earth, I see that this is the one thing needed: to be perfect with Him, wholly and entirely given up to Him. Wholly for God is the keynote of perfection.

TALK VS. POWER

For the kingdom of God is not a matter of talk but of power.
1 CORINTHIANS 4:20 NIV

Do you know any big talkers? They boast about their talents, their connections, their income, and their effect on women. If you have a story, they have a bigger one. If you have a question, they have the answer—though you might sense that it's not entirely right.

The apostle Paul dealt with people like that in the church at Corinth, people who were actually questioning his spiritual authority. But Paul had been specifically chosen by God to be the "apostle to the Gentiles" (Galatians 2:8 NIV), serving people like these Corinthians. Paul chided the church, ultimately telling them, "The kingdom of God is not a matter of talk but of power."

There's plenty of chatter in our world today, some of it even in the church. If that wearies or frustrates you, remember that it doesn't truly represent God's kingdom. Real faith is power—answered prayers, changed lives, eternal blessings. God wants these things for you. Seek Him first, and all the other things fall into place (Matthew 6:33).

SLOW TO ANGER

The LORD is slow to anger but great in power.

NAHUM 1:3 NIV

Do you consider yourself a patient person who isn't easily provoked? Or are you someone who sometimes finds himself emotionally "on edge"—impatient with others and given to becoming angry, even over small offenses?

Today's verse tells us that God is "slow to anger," meaning that He is patient with us, His imperfect but beloved people. And He wants us also to be slow to anger. The New Testament writer James made this very clear: "Everyone should be quick to listen, slow to speak and slow to become angry, because human anger does not produce the righteousness that God desires" (James 1:19–20 NIV).

Are you, like Jesus, slow to anger? Controlling your emotions will save you a lot of trouble in this life and help you avoid leaving a wake of hurt behind you. How much better to benefit others as you love them the way God does.

THE MAJESTIC, GRACIOUS GOD

"Heaven is my throne, and the earth is my footstool. Where is the house you will build for me? Where will my resting place be?"

ISAIAH 66:1 NIV

We should all recognize the danger of human pride. How often have we ruined a good deed by elevating ourselves over the God who empowers our works?

The prophet Isaiah wrote that God doesn't need our assistance—at all. The entire universe cannot contain His power and holiness, so how could we possibly benefit Him? What could we ever do to appease Him?

As Isaiah said elsewhere, "All our righteous acts are like filthy rags" (64:6 NIV), so we should never try to tell ourselves that we are earning God's respect. Rather, God freely transfers His righteousness to us when we accept Jesus' sacrifice by faith.

That is solely the work of our majestic, gracious God.

CLASSICS: CHARLES H. SPURGEON

OUR GOD IS PATIENT

He was oppressed, and he was afflicted, yet he opened not his mouth: he is brought as a lamb to the slaughter, and as a sheep before her shearers is dumb, so he openeth not his mouth.

ISAIAH 53:7 KJV

Our Lord was dumb and opened not His mouth against His adversaries and did not accuse one of them of cruelty or injustice. They slandered Him, but He replied not; false witnesses arose, but He answered them not. . . .

Jesus lets not fall a word against anybody, though they are doing everything that malice can invent against Him. For Pilate He even makes a half apology, "He that delivered me unto thee hath the greater sin." One would have thought He must have spoken when they spat in His face. . .or smote Him on the face with the palms of their hands. . . . But, no; He speaketh not. He brings no accusation to His Father. . . . There was no display of power, or rather there was so great a display of power over Himself that He did not use His might against His bitterest foes; He restrained Omnipotence itself with a strength which never can be measured, for His mighty love availed even to restrain divine wrath.

A GOD OF HONESTY

The Lord detests dishonest scales,
but accurate weights find favor with him.

PROVERBS 11:1 NIV

In ancient markets, merchants commonly used scales to measure out the weight of items customers wanted to purchase. An honest scale brought trust to the transaction, but dishonest sellers used hollowed-out weights or deceptively heavy weights to take advantage of their customers.

That's the picture behind the verse above. Dishonesty in any form displeases God. He sets the standard for honesty and fairness. He never lies or cheats, and He expects the same behavior from His people. As with any sin, He's willing to forgive dishonesty and injustice. But His desire moving forward is honesty, fairness, and truth. God can show you how to demonstrate all three.

ROOTED IN GOD

*A man will not stand by doing what is wrong, but the
root of those who are right with God will not be moved.*

PROVERBS 12:3 NLV

A tumbleweed grows fast on its shallow roots. The
result is a plant that doesn't stay rooted in the ground.
It serves little purpose other than to annoy people who
encounter it on a windy day.

God wants you to heed and obey His Word for
He knows that when you don't, you'll become much
like a tumbleweed. You may show some growth, but
because you aren't rooted in scripture, sooner or later
you will be blown around.

When you choose to follow God's laws, you're
more like a tree growing beside a stream. Your roots
are well fed, well watered, and deep, and they will
keep you in place even during the wildest storms.
Root yourself deeply in God's Word, and you will
always stand strong.

OUR RESCUING REDEEMER

*"I am the Lord your God, who rescued you from
the land of Egypt, the place of your slavery."*

EXODUS 20:2 NLT

God sets captives free. He did it for Israel when they were slaves in Egypt. He did it in the times of the judges when Israel cried out for deliverance from conquering nations. Most impressive of all, He did it on the cross when Jesus died and rose again to liberate sinners from sin's captivity.

When Jesus paid the price of sin on the cross, the freedom He bought for you wasn't so you would return to your chains. He set you free so you could follow Him!

We serve the God who rescues sinners from slavery. Do you recognize Him as the master He is, or are you being mastered by the sin He has freed you from?

CLASSICS: D. L. MOODY

GOD IS NEAR

And he said, Go forth, and stand upon the mount before the LORD. And, behold, the LORD passed by, and a great and strong wind rent the mountains, and brake in pieces the rocks before the LORD; but the LORD was not in the wind: and after the wind an earthquake; but the LORD was not in the earthquake: and after the earthquake a fire; but the LORD was not in the fire: and after the fire a still small voice.

1 KINGS 19:11–12 KJV

It is as a still small voice that God speaks to His children. Some people are trying to find out just how far heaven is away. There is one thing we know about it; that is, that is not so far away but that God can hear us when we pray. I do not believe there has ever been a tear shed for sin since Adam's fall in Eden to the present time, but God has witnessed it. He is not too far from earth for us to go to Him; and if there is a sigh that comes from a burdened heart today, God will hear that sigh. If there is a cry coming up from a heart broken on account of sin, God will hear that cry. He is not so far away, heaven is not so far away, as to be inaccessible to the smallest child.

PRAYING IN GOD'S SPIRIT

*And pray in the Spirit on all occasions with all kinds of
prayers and requests. With this in mind, be alert and
always keep on praying for all the Lord's people.*

EPHESIANS 6:18 NIV

What does Paul mean by urging us to pray "in the
Spirit"? We find the core truth of this shorthand phrase
near the middle of the letter to the Ephesian church: "I
pray that out of his glorious riches he may strengthen
you with power through his Spirit in your inner being"
(Ephesians 3:16 NIV). Other verses describing God's
strengthening "power" in us include Ephesians 1:19,
3:7–9, 3:14–21, and 6:10–20.

It quickly becomes apparent that Ephesians 6:18
can be understood to mean, "And pray with the power
of the Holy Spirit within you on all occasions. . . ."

Praying "in the Spirit" isn't boring. It's electric!

GOD ALWAYS KNOWS

*The Lord is watching everywhere, keeping his
eye on both the evil and the good.*

PROVERBS 15:3 NLT

There is nothing done that God cannot see, nothing that startles Him. He can't be taken by surprise and He never worries.

When you do something good and right, you don't have to wonder whether God knows. He does—because He always pays attention. He even knows why you chose to do good. God also knows when you make choices with evil intentions. He knows why you chose evil.

Some people believe God only observes what we do in order to punish us. But He pays attention to all our actions, words, and thoughts because He loves us. God always wants to bring us back to His side and keep us there.

GOD'S JEALOUSY

"You must not bow down to them or worship them, for I, the Lord your God, am a jealous God who will not tolerate your affection for any other gods. I lay the sins of the parents upon their children; the entire family is affected— even children in the third and fourth generations of those who reject me. But I lavish unfailing love for a thousand generations on those who love me and obey my commands".

EXODUS 20:5–6 NLT

God designed you to crave water when you're thirsty. Your mouth may want a cola, but what you need is water.

In the same way, God has created you to thirst for His presence. Your sinful body may want to slake that thirst with lesser things, but what you need is God.

What does this have to do with God being jealous? He knows your cravings will not be satisfied by lesser gods. He alone wants to be the One you crave, because He is the only One who can satisfy.

CLASSICS: D. L. MOODY

OUR MOTTO: NOTHING IS TOO HARD FOR GOD

Ah Lord God! behold, thou hast made the heaven and the earth by thy great power and stretched out arm, and there is nothing too hard for thee.

JEREMIAH 32:17 KJV

Jeremiah prayed and said: "Ah, Lord God! behold thou hast made the heaven and the earth by thy great power and stretched out arm, and there is nothing too hard for thee." Nothing is too hard for God; that is a good thing to take for a motto.

I believe this is a time of great blessing in the world, and we may expect great things. While the blessing is falling all around let us arise and share in it. God has said, "Call unto Me, and I will answer thee, and show thee great and mighty things which thou knowest not." Now let us call on the Lord; and let us pray that it may be done for Christ's sake—not our own.

GOD KNOWS ALL SECRETS

Even Death and Destruction hold no secrets from the Lord. How much more does he know the human heart!

PROVERBS 15:11 NLT

The devil may believe he can deceive God, but the Lord knows fact from fiction, truth from lies, wisdom from foolishness. God knows Satan's end story, that all the devil's secrets will be exposed.

Since God knows His adversary so well, it should come as no surprise that He is fully acquainted with your heart. The Lord knows how its decisions are formed and shaped. He knows the desperation and wickedness. He knows the hope and transformation. He knows everything—and it's to your ultimate advantage that He does.

You may fool some people, but you can't hide your secrets from God. And because He knows everything about you, He can help you in ways that truly meet your needs and keep you close to Him.

GOD'S GOOD NEWS

*Look, there on the mountains, the feet of one
who brings good news, who proclaims peace!*

NAHUM 1:15 NIV

The Bible as a whole can be seen as the intricate story of God bringing the good news of salvation through Jesus Christ to the world. This story didn't begin with the birth of Jesus as it is told in the four Gospels. It was lovingly crafted much earlier than that, starting with God's hint of a Savior way back in the Garden of Eden (see Genesis 3:14–15).

God has given us the responsibility—and the privilege—of taking this good news into our world. The prophet Isaiah elaborated on Nahum's message above when he wrote, "How beautiful on the mountains are the feet of those who bring good news, who proclaim peace, who bring good tidings, who proclaim salvation, who say to Zion, 'Your God reigns!' " (Isaiah 52:7 NIV).

Salvation through Jesus is the greatest news in human history. What can you do today to make sure people around you hear it?

GOD WANTS TO HEAR FROM YOU

*Don't worry about anything; instead, pray about everything.
Tell God what you need, and thank him for all he has done.
Then you will experience God's peace, which exceeds
anything we can understand. His peace will guard your
hearts and minds as you live in Christ Jesus.*

PHILIPPIANS 4:6–7 NLT

How should you pray today? God wants us to pray "about everything," so if it's in your heart and mind, pray about it. Yes, God already knows about it, but He wants you to lay it before Him humbly, in complete surrender.

Jesus could have healed the blind, the leprous, and the deathly ill at the start of each new week. Instead, He waited to be asked. His question was "What do you want Me to do for you?" (see Matthew 20:32, Mark 10:36 and 10:51, and Luke 18:41). Imagine the Lord asking *you* that same question. In a sense, He already is, and He wants to hear back from you. How will you answer Him today?

CLASSICS: CHARLES H. SPURGEON

SEEK THE LORD YOUR GOD

Now set your heart and your soul to seek the LORD your God.
1 CHRONICLES 22:19 KJV

Our first enquiry is, "What are they to seek?" Beloved friends, I say to you, as David said to the princes of Israel, "Seek the Lord your God." Do it by endeavoring to obey Him in everything. Let it be our study to test everything that we do by God's holy Word. Let us not willfully sin, either in commission or in omission. Let us be very particular to seek out the will of the Lord, so as to fulfill not only commands which are plain, but those about which there is a question. . . .

Therefore let us pledge ourselves unto God to live more and more watchfully, seeking the Lord with our heart and soul in everything—in private, in the family, in business, and in the house of God. . . . O Christian, set your heart to this, that the Lord Jesus is your absolute Lord and Master; and that, at every point, you will scrupulously endeavor to do His will, yielding a cheerful obedience as the fruit of the Spirit within your soul!

GOD'S NAME IS A FORTIFIED TOWER

The name of the Lord is a fortified tower;
the righteous run to it and are safe.

PROVERBS 18:10 NIV

Think of an ancient castle. It's a fortress with a moat for defense and a high tower for offense. Once inside, you find protection. You can relax because nothing outside can break through to you. You have access to the powerful man who owns the place.

This is a word picture of access to God's great name. It is a tower in a fortified, impenetrable castle. Protection is found here. Just run to God, who welcomes you in.

As a follower of Jesus Christ, you can believe that this tower is available to you for rest, refreshment, and rejuvenation. "The righteous run to it and are safe."

WILLING TO REPEAT HIMSELF

The Lord said to Moses, "Chisel out two stone tablets like the first ones, and I will write on them the words that were on the first tablets, which you broke."

EXODUS 34:1 NIV

After Moses led the Israelites out of Egypt, they camped in the wilderness of Sinai. Even before they had the particulars of the forthcoming covenant with God, the Israelites agreed to serve Him faithfully (see Exodus 19:1–8). Moses went up Mount Sinai to get the details that God personally carved onto two tablets (see Exodus 31:18).

But when the people felt Moses was gone a little too long, they made a golden calf to worship, breaking the covenant before it was even delivered. Moses was so angry that he broke the stone tablets. Then God called Moses back up the mountain and gave him another set.

Even when we break God's laws, He is willing to repeat Himself. He lovingly calls us back into His presence and reiterates His love for us. Over and over again.

GOD'S POWER EXALTS THE HUMBLE

Humble yourselves therefore under the mighty hand of God, that he may exalt you in due time.

1 PETER 5:6 KJV

Have you ever noticed the Bible's paradoxes? The apostle Paul wrote that when he was weak, he was strong (2 Corinthians 12:10)—because God's power could flow through him. Jesus taught that "he that is least among you all, the same shall be great" (Luke 9:48 KJV)—indicating the value God puts on humility. Similar ideas come through the apostle Peter in today's scripture.

Humbling ourselves at present leads to our exaltation by God in the future. This exaltation will occur "in due time"—maybe in this life, maybe in eternity. Either way, we can expect it to be very, very good.

Just never forget the prerequisite: "humble yourselves." When we acknowledge God's mighty hand in our lives, He will apply that power to our weaknesses. That brings honor to Himself and benefit to us.

CLASSICS: D. L. MOODY

HOW GOD LOVES US!

For God so loved the world, that he gave his only begotten Son, that whosoever believeth in him should not perish, but have everlasting life.

JOHN 3:16 KJV

No mother's love is to be compared with the love of God; it does not measure the height or the depth of God's love. No mother in this world ever loved her child as God loves you and me.

Think of the love that God must have had when He gave His Son to die for the world. After I became a father and for years had an only son, as I looked at my boy I thought of the Father giving His Son to die; and it seemed to me as if it required more love for the Father to give His Son than for the Son to die.

Oh, the love God must have had for the world when He gave His Son to die for it!

THE GOD WHO KNOWS YOU

Before I formed thee in the belly I knew thee.

JEREMIAH 1:5 KJV

As Christians, we should already realize that God knows everything about us. But have you ever reflected on the fact that He knew you personally long before you even existed?

Imagine God spreading out the cosmos, sprinkling it with stars and planets, all while thinking of *you*. And He didn't just know your name—He knew every thought you'd ever have, including the one you're thinking now. He orchestrated your birth and upbringing so you'd have a chance to know and experience Him.

As Jesus agonized on the cross, your personal decision to follow Him was firmly in His mind, strengthening His resolve to endure such suffering.

Once we understand these truths, Jesus' instruction to "take therefore no thought for the morrow" (Matthew 6:34 KJV) makes much more sense. God knows you and cares about your needs—and He's been waiting since time began just to fulfill them!

GOD LOVES COMPASSIONATE ACTION

*He who shuts his ears to the cry of the poor
will also cry himself and not be answered.*

PROVERBS 21:13 NLV

You take care of yourself, right? You might take care
of parents or children or grandchildren. It's a big job,
and when you do it, you might think you've done all
you can—and all God has called you to.

But when you hear that someone else needs help,
it's easy to come up with reasons why you can't assist.
These reasons usually involve time, money, or the belief
that someone else will (or should) jump in.

God's heart, though, is to intervene. It's what He's
done for you, and it's what He wants you to do for
others. He wants you to step into someone else's pain
and relieve it in any way you can. The offer of time,
money, or other resources can be a gift from God
through you to someone who needs hope. Hard as it
may seem at the time, there will be a reward—God's
great and generous reward.

JESUS GIVES US STRENGTH

I can do all things because Christ gives me the strength.

PHILIPPIANS 4:13 NLV

This is one of the Bible's most inspirational verses. The primary meaning is finding contentment in the Lord in every circumstance. With that in mind, let's unpack this inspiring truth.

In His infinite sovereignty, God has unlimited power. *He* can do anything and everything. In turn, the Lord wants us to do many good things. Yet without Him, of course, we can do nothing. For us do anything of eternal worth, therefore, we need God to dwell in us and we need to pray for His will to be done.

In context, today's verse means that we can overcome any and all of life's difficulties, accomplish God's will, and enjoy contentment, all because of Jesus Christ's power at work in and through us.

No less than the Lord God, creator of the heavens and earth, longs to work through you. Right now, ask God to show you His will today. Then say yes!

CLASSICS: ANDREW MURRAY

BE HOLY, BE BLESSED

And when he had consulted with the people, he appointed singers unto the LORD, and that should praise the beauty of holiness, as they went out before the army, and to say, Praise the LORD; for his mercy endureth for ever.

2 CHRONICLES 20:21 KJV

We are to worship Him "in the beauty of holiness," "to sing praise at the remembrance of His Holiness"; it is only in the spirit of worship and praise and joy that we fully can know God as holy. Much more, it is only under the inspiration of adoring love and joy that we can ourselves be made holy. It is as we cease from all fear and anxiety, from all strain and effort, and rest with singing in what Jesus is in His finished work as our sanctification, as we rest and rejoice in Him, that we shall be made partakers of His holiness. It is the day of rest, that is the day God has blessed, the day of blessing and gladness; and it is the day He blessed that is His holy day. Holiness and blessedness are inseparable.

NO DISCRIMINATION WITH GOD

*The poor and the oppressor have this in common—
the LORD gives sight to the eyes of both.*

PROVERBS 29:13 NLT

It's easy to accept the fact that our compassionate God makes Himself known to the poor, the disadvantaged, and the disabled. But what about those in positions of leadership and power who oppress others?

You might think that the oppressors should not be recipients of God's blessings. But the verse above says that these two examples of humanity receive the *same* blessings from God. This New Living Translation suggests that they share the gift of sight. Another version says they share light.

The Bible also says that God sends the rain to all, but there's also food, water, air, and love. God does not discriminate in His care of humanity. The poor and the oppressors both need God's love because both need God. Let that inform how you see the people He loves.

GOD'S APPOINTED DESTINATION

"Write down the revelation and make it plain on tablets so that a herald may run with it. For the revelation awaits an appointed time; it speaks of the end and will not prove false. Though it linger, wait for it; it will certainly come and will not delay."

HABAKKUK 2:2–3 NIV

Habakkuk had a bone to pick with God. Like a disgruntled customer returning a meal that is not to his liking, he went before God and boldly laid out his complaint: "Why are you silent while the wicked swallow up those more righteous than themselves? You have made people like the fish in the sea, like the sea creatures that have no ruler. The wicked foe pulls all of them up with hooks, he catches them in his net. . .and so he rejoices and is glad" (1:13–15 NIV). God replied to Habakkuk's challenge with a reminder that the end He has prepared is coming.

Rather than constantly whining, "Are we there yet?" maybe we should stop grabbing for the wheel and just allow God to drive us to the destination *He* knows is best.

GOD'S EXTENDED NAME

And the Lord passed by before him, and proclaimed, The Lord, The Lord God, merciful and gracious, longsuffering, and abundant in goodness and truth, keeping mercy for thousands, forgiving iniquity and transgression and sin, and that will by no means clear the guilty; visiting the iniquity of the fathers upon the children, and upon the children's children, unto the third and to the fourth generation.

EXODUS 34:6–7 KJV

In Exodus 3:14, God told Moses His name: "I Am." In today's passage, God goes on to describe Himself in greater detail.

The Lord is merciful, gracious, patient, good, and true. When He passed by Moses, telling him His extended name, Moses was changed, and his face shone with the light of God's identity.

When God introduces Himself to you, when you feel His mercy, grace, patience, goodness, and truth, you cannot help but shine with His identity too. Not only will God's presence show on your face, it'll show up in your deeds.

Shine on!

CLASSICS: ANDREW MURRAY

GOD HEARS YOUR CRIES

For the people shall dwell in Zion at Jerusalem: thou shalt weep no more: he will be very gracious unto thee at the voice of thy cry; when he shall hear it, he will answer thee.

ISAIAH 30:19 KJV

I desire at this time to set forth the graciousness of God and His readiness to listen to the cry of the needy, with the hope that some here present who may have forgotten this, to whom it may be a time of need, may hear it and be encouraged to say, "I will arise and go to my Father."

It is joy to me to hope that it will be so, but I remember with sadness that if I should be helped to set this forth clearly, and if any of you who are in trouble should afterwards refuse to trust in the Lord, your alienation will be aggravated, your sin will become still more crying. He who will not trust when he knows that the Lord will be gracious to him sins against his own soul and plunges himself in sevenfold wrath.

If the Lord saith that he will be very gracious at the voice of your cry, what must be your doom if you will not cry?

WHAT GOD WANTS US TO PURSUE

To the person who pleases him, God gives wisdom, knowledge and happiness, but to the sinner he gives the task of gathering and storing up wealth to hand it over to the one who pleases God. This too is meaningless, a chasing after the wind.

ECCLESIASTES 2:26 NIV

Ecclesiastes is one of the most interesting books of the Bible. It was penned by King Solomon later in his life, and it's filled with negative word pictures. It constantly looks at life as something less desirable the older you get. Many of these word pictures describe things the king once thought important but ultimately concluded were meaningless at best.

The scripture above begins with the value of God's gift of wisdom and contrasts it with those who spend their lives accumulating money that they leave to someone else when they die. The king recognized meaningless of this latter pursuit.

Wisdom is a benefit to you and those you share it with. Money is gathered and lost personally, but the wisdom God freely gives has lifetime benefits.

WHO IS JESUS?

Christ is the visible image of the invisible God. He existed before anything was created and is supreme over all creation, for through him God created everything in the heavenly realms and on earth.

COLOSSIANS 1:15–16 NLT

Christians believe Jesus Christ created everything. But that's not all. They believe Jesus came to earth and lived here for more than thirty years. They believe Jesus is eternally and fully God and more than two thousand years ago he became fully human too.

They believe Jesus performed many great miracles during His last three years here on earth. They believe Jesus proclaimed good news to humanity. They believe Jesus was crucified on a Roman cross in our place for our sins. They believe Jesus forgives all sins of those who trust Him.

They believe Jesus gives the right to become children of God to all who receive Him. They believe Jesus offers eternal life to all who place their faith in Him. Finally, they believe Jesus is coming back to earth one day.

Are you a Christian? If so, celebrate God's great love. If not, ask God today to make you part of His family.

GOD'S BLESSED WORK

*I know that every man who eats and drinks sees
good in all his work. It is the gift of God.*

ECCLESIASTES 3:13 NLV

Many think of work as something they *have* to do,
something to endure, something that prevents them
from doing things they would rather do. But there's
plenty of biblical evidence suggesting that work is
a gift from God, something in which we men can
find satisfaction.

Your work should be a representation of God at
work in the world. He keeps steady at His tasks and
completes what He starts. He doesn't cut corners,
and He doesn't complain that the job is too hard.
God simply works.

Perhaps He wants you to experience the same
joy He has in ensuring that the finished work is well
done. If you follow Christ, you should be viewed as
an exceptional hire because you see good in all your
work—and you work for reasons beyond a paycheck,
a weekend, or your next big purchase.

CLASSICS: CHARLES H. SPURGEON

GOD IS READY TO PARDON

But thou art a God ready to pardon, gracious and merciful, slow to anger, and of great kindness, and forsookest them not.

NEHEMIAH 9:17 KJV

I would call your attention to the expression, "a God ready to pardon," not a God who may possibly pardon; neither a God who upon strong persuasion and earnest pleadings may, at length, be induced to forgive; not one who, perchance, at some remote period after we have undergone a long purgation may manifest a mercy which is now in the background, but a God "ready to pardon"—willing and more than willing— ready, standing prepared or, to use another scriptural expression, "waiting to be gracious." We have a God who stands like a host at a festival, which is all provided and prepared, saying, "My oxen and my fatlings are provided, all things are ready, come ye to the suppers." Not only are all things ready, but God Himself is ready, His own heart and hand all ready to bestow pardon upon the guilty ones who come before Him. There is forgiveness with Him that He may be feared.

FEAR VS. GOD

"If the LORD is pleased with us, he will lead us into that land, a land flowing with milk and honey, and will give it to us. Only do not rebel against the LORD. And do not be afraid of the people of the land, because we will devour them. Their protection is gone, but the LORD is with us. Do not be afraid of them."

NUMBERS 14:8–9 NIV

Fear is the thief of rationality. We cannot think clearly when fear rules our lives.

Despite the miracles they'd seen in Egypt and the provision of manna and the covenant they made with God at Mount Sinai, the Israelites were afraid of the promised land's gigantic inhabitants. Obviously, they weren't thinking clearly.

When life seems scary to you, when God calls you into your own promised land, fear may seem like a reasonable response. It isn't. When you are doing what God wants, you needn't fear any giants in your promised land. Let *them* fear the God who goes before you!

GOD WANTS GOOD COMMUNICATION

As you enter the house of God, keep your ears open and your mouth shut. It is evil to make mindless offerings to God. Don't make rash promises, and don't be hasty in bringing matters before God. After all, God is in heaven, and you are here on earth. So let your words be few.

ECCLESIASTES 5:1–2 NLT

King Solomon knew that God should be honored. He shouldn't be treated as a buddy we hang out with after school or work. Solomon wanted to honor God when he prayed by saying the things God had given him to say.

Solomon was even aware that there was a time to be quiet. He was not suggesting that we not pray but was actually advocating for thoughtful and honorable communication with God.

Pray when you have something to say. The end result does not have a minimum or maximum word or time limit. The message was to resist being hasty and impulsive. Speak to God in prayer often, but remember that more words do not always mean better communication.

JESUS' INFINITE WISDOM AND UNDERSTANDING

In Christ are hidden all the riches of wisdom and understanding.

COLOSSIANS 2:3 NLV

When we think about who Jesus Christ is, we need to remember He is omniscient, or all-knowing. This doesn't just mean He's mastered all the facts of the universe. He knows much, much more.

Remember phone books? A million facts, but none that could change your life. By themselves, facts are pretty inconsequential. Our Lord possesses all of those facts, but within the context of all discernment, insight, understanding, and wisdom—in way-above-our-heads ways. In other words, "God alone knows," multiplied by infinity and eternity.

Why in the world are we ever tempted to think we know better than the Lord? We know better than Him how to run our lives? Not a chance! Let's humbly acknowledge His higher, heavenly wisdom and ways today.

CLASSICS: CHARLES H. SPURGEON

WE ALL HAVE JOB'S GOD

So the Lord blessed the latter end of Job more than his beginning: for he had fourteen thousand sheep, and six thousand camels, and a thousand yoke of oxen, and a thousand she asses. He had also seven sons and three daughters.

JOB 42:12–13 KJV

We are not all like Job, but we all have Job's God. Though we have neither risen to Job's wealth, nor will, probably, ever sink to Job's poverty, yet there is the same God above us if we be high, and the same God with His everlasting arms beneath us if we be brought low; and what the Lord did for Job He will do for us, not precisely in the same form, but in the same spirit, and with like design. If, therefore, we are brought low tonight, let us be encouraged with the thought that God will turn again our captivity; and let us entertain the hope that after the time of trial shall be over, we shall be richer, especially in spiritual things, than ever we were before.

WEAK TO STRONG

*I take pleasure in infirmities, in reproaches,
in necessities, in persecutions, in distresses for
Christ's sake: for when I am weak, then am I strong.*

2 CORINTHIANS 12:10 KJV

Good news: If you don't feel like you're up to the task,
you're right where God wants you.

Consider the apostle Paul, who had been blessed by
God with a vision of heaven. "Caught up into paradise,"
Paul heard "unspeakable words, which it is not lawful
for a man to utter" (2 Corinthians 12:4 KJV). He might
have used such an experience to silence his critics and
overpower those who doubted his calling. But instead
Paul focused on his "infirmities" (verse 5), the "thorn
in the flesh" (verse 7) that kept him humble.

These infirmities, in fact, were a source of pleasure
for Paul. His own weaknesses, the insults of opponents,
the lack of vital supplies, the arrests and beatings he
endured for following Jesus—each and every one of
these things made him strong. How? Reaching the
end of his own strength allowed Paul to see "that the
power of Christ may rest upon me" (verse 9 KJV).

WHAT GOD DESIRES

He has shown you, O mortal, what is good. And what does the Lord require of you? To act justly and to love mercy and to walk humbly with your God.

MICAH 6:8 NIV

The minor prophets are among the least read, least understood books in all the Bible. It's not surprising, considering their message so directly addresses the injustice, suffering, unfaithfulness, corruption, and arrogance of God's children. They remind us over and over again that all of us have sinned.

Why would God forgive such messed-up people?

Hard as it is to believe, it seems that He actually *wants* to. God desires fellowship with us—and that we have that same fellowship with each other. Micah's heartfelt cry reminds us of this: "Who is a God like you, who pardons sin and forgives the transgression of the remnant of his inheritance? You do not stay angry forever but delight to show mercy" (Micah 7:18 NIV).

We have all been forgiven of so much. Let us never forget to extend that same kindness to those around us.

GOD HATES HYPOCRISY

"I hate, I despise your religious festivals;
your assemblies are a stench to me."

AMOS 5:21 NIV

In the book of Amos, God's condemnation of hypocrisy reaches a level of blistering intensity rarely found elsewhere. The Israelites, in order to mask their sin, were relying on the outward show of sacrifices and feasts to save them—an attitude that God hated.

We are often quick to point out hypocrisy in others, but do we turn the same critical lens on ourselves? How often do we allow our own good deeds and church attendance to distract us from the strains that exist in our relationship with God?

Christianity is not just a list of things we must or must not do—it is a change of heart, a replacement of our selfishness with sincere love toward God and others. Once we realize this, "Justice [will] roll on like a river, righteousness like a never-failing stream" (Amos 5:24 NIV).

CLASSICS: D. L. MOODY

CHRIST BLESSES THE NEEDY

Even so it is not the will of your Father which is in heaven, that one of these little ones should perish.

MATTHEW 18:14 KJV

When Christ commenced His ministry in the wonderful sermon on the mount there was blessing, blessing, blessing upon blessing. He came to bless man, not to condemn man. Zacchaeus needed blessing, and He gave it him. Poor blind Bartimaeus needed blessing, and He gave it him.

If there is some Zacchaeus, some poor blind beggar now needing blessing, Christ will bless that needy one. The Son of man is come for that purpose; He left heaven and a throne for that. And so the vilest man can be saved if he will. The Lord is able and willing to save. "He is come to seek and to save that which was lost."

GOD GIVES GOOD DAYS AND BAD DAYS

When times are good, be happy; but when times are bad, consider this: God has made the one as well as the other.

ECCLESIASTES 7:14 NIV

There will be good days in this life, and they will make you feel blessed. But there will be bad days that make you wonder what you've done wrong. Long before Jesus promised trouble in this world, Solomon spoke this simple truth: God promises us good and bad days alike.

If you wonder why God would allow people to experience bad with good, you need to understand that God does things very different from the way we do. From a practical standpoint, bad days can clarify your focus on God, encourage prayer, and invite trust.

Metaphorically speaking, if good days are sunshine and bad days are rain, then it might make sense that both are needed for growth.

GOD'S WRATH

*And fire came out from the Lord and consumed
the 250 men who were offering the incense.*

NUMBERS 16:35 NIV

The wrath of God is a terrible thing for those who incur it. . .but it's also a wonderful thing. If God didn't take seriously the consequences He laid out in His covenant with humanity, He would be violating His own rules, which He will not do. Yes, God is merciful to those who repent, but He is also swift to judge those who refuse Him.

Today, in a world redeemed by the blood of Jesus, we are still born under sin's curse and destined for God's wrath until we surrender our lives to Him. When we do, the Father's wrath is turned from us to His Son, who paid for our sins on the cross. God's love made a way for His children, satisfying the rules He made at the cost to Himself.

Praise God for both His wrath and His mercy!

THE ETERNAL TRUTH OF JESUS

*So then, just as you received Christ Jesus as Lord,
continue to live your lives in him, rooted and built up
in him, strengthened in the faith as you were taught.*

COLOSSIANS 2:6–7 NIV

In Colossians, the apostle Paul contrasts the eternal truths of Christianity with the false and fleeting philosophies of the ancient world. Each of the eternal truths was clearly espoused by Jesus Christ and His apostles.

What's more, every branch of Christianity down through the centuries and around the world has borne witness to these eternal truths. Colossae's "college-town questions" had no more impact on core Christian truths than an ant walking on a massive oak tree.

So we should not be afraid to ask questions. Tough questions. Critical questions. Doubting questions. Nor should we be afraid to hear questions from struggling saints, skeptics, agnostics, and even atheists.

Questions—even those that shock, shake, or stump us—cannot damage, diminish, or destroy the eternal truth of Jesus.

THE REWARD IS COMING

One thing have I desired of the LORD, that will I seek after; that I may dwell in the house of the LORD all the days of my life, to behold the beauty of the LORD, and to enquire in his temple.

PSALM 27:4 KJV

One glimpse of Christ will pay us for all we are called upon to endure here—to see the King in His beauty, to be in the presence of the King! And then, oh! The sweet thought, we shall be like Him when we see Him! And we shall see Him in His beauty; we shall see Him high and exalted. When He was down here on earth it was the time of His humiliation, when He was cast out from the world, spit upon and rejected; but God hath exalted Him and put Him at the right hand of power, and there He is now, and there we shall see Him by and by. A few more tears, a few more shadows, and then the voice of God shall say, "Come up hither," and into the presence of the King we shall go.

GOD KNOWS LITERALLY EVERYTHING

I saw all the work of God and knew that man cannot even think of all that is done under the sun. Even if man tries hard to find out, he will not be able to. Even if a wise man says he knows, he does not.

ECCLESIASTES 8:17 NLV

No matter how much you know, there will always be more to know. No matter how much you discover, there will always be more to discover. No matter how deeply you search, there will always be more to search.

God has done more, created more, and thought of more than you ever will. The advances you hear about in the news today were known to Him infinitely long ago, before the creation of the world. There is no new discovery for God to make. So learn from God, and be subject to change. He gives wisdom, and that will transform what you think you know.

YOUR BENEFACTOR IN HEAVEN

Whatever you do, work at it with all your heart, as working for the Lord, not for human masters, since you know that you will receive an inheritance from the Lord as a reward. It is the Lord Christ you are serving.

COLOSSIANS 3:23–24 NIV

What does the apostle Paul mean by the shorthand phrase "an inheritance"? In this epistle, we find the core truth early: "giving joyful thanks to the Father, who has qualified you to share in the inheritance of his holy people in the kingdom of light. For he [the Father] has rescued us from the dominion of darkness and brought us into the kingdom of the Son he loves" (Colossians 1:12–13 NIV).

It quickly becomes apparent that Colossians 3:23–24 can be understood to mean, "You will receive, as your reward, the inheritance of the saints of light in the kingdom of God's beloved Son. You are serving God's beloved Son, the Lord Jesus Christ."

What a thrilling reward God has for you to enjoy—for all eternity.

GOD IS TRUSTWORTHY

"God is not a man, so he does not lie. He is not human, so he does not change his mind. Has he ever spoken and failed to act? Has he ever promised and not carried it through?"

NUMBERS 23:19 NLT

God isn't just truthful; He *is* truth. It is not in His character to lie. And in His eternal omniscience, God knows what will happen before it happens. He doesn't need to change His mind about anything because nothing surprises Him. God's plans cannot be thwarted. His promises are never at risk because nothing can come between them and their fruition.

God's trustworthiness is critical to faith. If He failed to keep His promises, He would either be a liar unworthy of our trust or He would be too weak to keep them. In either case, He would cease to be God.

But He *is* God. He *is* trustworthy. And when He tells us that He loves us, we can take Him at His word.

GOD'S SPIRIT MAKES US GLAD

Thou lovest righteousness, and hatest wickedness:
therefore God, thy God, hath anointed thee with
the oil of gladness above thy fellows.

PSALM 45:7 KJV

The divine Spirit has many attributes, and his benign influences operate in divers ways, bestowing upon us benefits of various kinds, too numerous for us to attempt to catalogue them. Amongst these is His comforting and cheering influence. "The fruit of the Spirit is joy." In Acts 13:52 we read, "The disciples were filled with joy and with the Holy Ghost." Wherever He comes as an anointing, whether upon the Lord or upon His people, upon the Christ or the Christians, upon the Anointed or upon those whom He anoints, in every case the ultimate result is joy and peace. On the head of our great High Priest He is joy, and this oil of gladness flows down to the skirts of His garments. To the Comforter, therefore, we ascribe "the oil of gladness."

GOD'S PROCLAMATION OF LOVE

Let him lead me to the banquet hall,
and let his banner over me be love.

SONG OF SOLOMON 2:4 NIV

Song of Solomon has two meanings. The first is a love letter written from King Solomon to his wife. But this book is also considered an allegory, a story with a second hidden meaning. In this case, it's the story of God's love for His people.

As an allegory, the verse above shows God celebrating you. The banquet and the banner are proclamations of God's love for you—and all His people.

God doesn't leave you wondering. His proclamations of love for you are also promises—and He never breaks His promises. Trouble will come in this life, but the God who is bigger than any trouble you will ever face will always be there for you.

Enjoy the banquet and the banner. They are your reminders of a very good, very loving God.

A HOPE-GIVING GOD

"But you, Bethlehem Ephrathah, though you are small among the clans of Judah, out of you will come for me one who will be ruler over Israel, whose origins are from of old, from ancient times."

MICAH 5:2 NIV

Micah 5:1 is a prophetic announcement that Israel would one day be dominated by foreign powers. But in the very next verse, God gave this message of hope through Micah: out of the tiny town of Bethlehem would come One who would be ruler of Israel.

Bethlehem was and is known as the City of David, for it was the hometown of Israel's greatest king. But Bethlehem wasn't a large or important city to the people of Israel. Despite its insignificance, however, God chose this little town as the birthplace of the Messiah, who will one day rule over Israel—and the entire world.

God loves to use the seemingly small and insignificant things to bring His people hope and comfort. He did it through the tiny town of Bethlehem, and He can do it for you too.

GOD STRENGTHENS OUR HEARTS

May the Lord make your love increase and overflow for each other and for everyone else, just as ours does for you. May he strengthen your hearts so that you will be blameless and holy in the presence of our God and Father when our Lord Jesus comes with all his holy ones.

1 THESSALONIANS 3:12–13 NIV

Thomas à Kempis's book *The Imitation of Christ*, especially its closing three chapters, speaks of the importance of beginning with the end in mind. That is, of thinking deeply and often when alone about the day of your death.

Do you want to finish this life well? Do you want to leave a good, godly, Christ-honoring legacy? If so, it's profoundly helpful to meditate on Kempis's question, "How do you want to meet God?"

How you live and think matters to the Lord. And He hasn't left you to navigate this life on your own. Through His Holy Spirit, God enables you to be the kind of man who looks forward to meeting Him, the guy who is "blameless and holy" in His presence.

CLASSICS: CHARLES H. SPURGEON

THE GLORIOUS ASCENT

Thou hast ascended on high, thou hast led captivity captive.

PSALM 68:18 KJV

Our Savior descended when He came to the manger of Bethlehem; and further descended when He became "a man of sorrows, and acquainted with grief." He descended lower still when He was obedient to death, even the death of the cross; and further yet when His dead body was laid in the grave. . . . Seeing He stood in their place and stead, He went as low as justice required that sinners should go who had dared to violate the law of God. The utmost abyss of desertion heard Him cry, "My God, my God, why hast thou forsaken me?" . . . On the third day He quitted the couch of the dead and rose to the light of the living. He had commenced His glorious ascent. To prove how real was His resurrection, He stayed on earth some forty days and showed Himself to many witnesses. Magdalene and James saw Him alone; the eleven beheld Him in their midst; the two on the road conversed with Him; five hundred brethren at once beheld Him. He gave infallible proofs that He was really risen from the dead, and these remain with us unto this day as historic facts.

GOD PROVIDES PROTECTION

*"Catch the foxes for us, the little foxes that are destroying
our grape-fields, for the flowers are on the vines."*

SONG OF SOLOMON 2:15 NLV

If the verse above reads to you like poetry, then you
have read it as was intended. The lessons learned in
Song of Solomon can rightfully be applied to marriage, but it is also appropriate to apply them to your
life in Christ.

In today's scripture, you get the picture of something vibrant, growing, and new—the grape-fields. But
predators have found their way in, seeking to destroy
the present growth and prevent future development.
When put in this nonpoetic way, it may sound a little
boring, but take this boring idea and reread the verse.
Does it make more sense? You should also be able to
see how the idea applies to both marriage and the
Christian life.

You can even rephrase the verse and use it as a
prayer to God asking for His protection as you grow.
It's a prayer He likes to answer.

OUR EXAMPLE OF TRUSTWORTHINESS

"If a man makes a promise to the Lord, or swears that he will keep his promise, he must not break his word. He must do all that he said he would do."

NUMBERS 30:2 NLV

God doesn't break His word to us, so we shouldn't break our word to Him.

There are two applications to this truth. First, we must be careful when we make promises to God. When God makes a promise, He has the advantage of knowing how His promises will play out through time. But we can't see the future. When we promise something without knowing if it is possible, we set ourselves up for failure.

Second, when we do make a promise, we would do well to keep it. God deserves our obedience, and by making a promise to Him, we invite Him to keep us accountable. Even when our promises are made to other people—not to God directly—they reflect on Him because we are God's children.

Be careful, and be trustworthy.

GOD'S MERCY IS GREAT

"We do not make requests of you because we are righteous, but because of your great mercy."

DANIEL 9:18 NIV

The prophet Daniel understood the consequences of sin. Not because he was particularly sinful—he was, in fact, one of the more devoted characters in scripture—but because his people's sin had led to the destruction of their nation. And Daniel himself had been carried away captive by the Babylonians.

Faithful in his work and blessed by his God, Daniel rose to leadership in his country of exile. When he read the prophecies of Jeremiah, Daniel learned the time frame of the present exile—and immediately turned to prayer.

"We have sinned and done wrong," he said, including himself in the confession. "We have been wicked and rebelled" (Daniel 9:5 NIV). Daniel implored God to turn His anger from His people, for the Lord's own sake. And then Daniel prayed the words of today's scripture. Nobody earns God's attention and help. We request them, humbly, acknowledging His great goodness.

This is a good line to add to our own prayers.

CLASSICS: JOHN WESLEY

GOD SAVES THE MEEK

Thou didst cause judgment to be heard from heaven; the earth feared, and was still, when God arose to judgment, to save all the meek of the earth. Selah.

PSALM 76:8–9 KJV

Suppose there were no God in the world; or, suppose He did not concern Himself with the children of men: But "when God ariseth to judgment, and to help all the meek upon earth," how doth He laugh all this heathen wisdom to scorn.... He takes a peculiar care to provide them with all things needful for life and godliness; He secures to them the provision He hath made in spite of the force, fraud, or malice of men; and what He secures He gives them richly to enjoy. It is sweet to them, be it little or much. As in patience they possess their souls, so they truly possess whatever God hath given them. They are always content, always pleased with what they have. It pleases them because it pleases God: So that while their heart, their desire, their joy is in heaven, they may truly be said to "inherit the earth."

THE LOWLY KING

Rejoice greatly, Daughter Zion! Shout, Daughter Jerusalem!
See, your king comes to you, righteous and victorious, lowly
and riding on a donkey, on a colt, the foal of a donkey.

ZECHARIAH 9:9 NIV

Humility is a character trait that many admire but few are willing to pursue. Often, in the heat of the moment, the passionate urge to defend our own honor overshadows any ideals we might have about humble submission.

As God Himself, the Creator and Sustainer of the universe, Jesus had every right to fulfill His disciples' expectations by establishing a mighty empire on earth. However, instead of straddling a white charger and leading an army to victory, Jesus rode into Jerusalem on a lowly donkey, symbolic of the humiliating fate that lay before Him.

Even when the world overlooks our achievements, we can trust God's promise to exalt us in due time (1 Peter 5:6). We might be lowly beggars now, but soon we will shine with Christ as kings.

GOD'S LOVE PROMISED

Place me like a seal over your heart, like a seal on your arm.
SONG OF SOLOMON 8:6 NLT

If this is both a statement from a wife to a husband and a Christian to God, then it speaks to intense vulnerability. In both, it's seeking confirmation of commitment. Does the husband love his wife enough to commit to walking with her through the hard, unpleasant, and difficult in life? Likewise, does God love you enough to commit to ongoing care through the hard, unpleasant, and difficult in life?

This verse is less a demand and more a plea. The need is for dependability, closeness, and companionship. Nothing about this is part-time. This passage echoes sentiments expressed elsewhere: "I am Yours, You are mine" (see Song of Solomon 2:16).

Use this request as a prayer. Be vulnerable enough to ask God for what you most need—someone who never leaves or abandons and whose love is a promise fulfilled.

GOD'S UNCHANGEABLE WORD

Do not add to what I command you and do not subtract from it, but keep the commands of the Lord your God that I give you.

DEUTERONOMY 4:2 NIV

God is the author of creation. He is the writer of His covenant with humanity. Everything He writes is perfect. It is humans who seek to change what God has written to better suit ourselves.

When the devil approached Adam and Eve in the garden, he asked a question that humanity has echoed many times since: "Did God really say. . . ?"

In giving us the Bible, His inspired Word, God recorded His unchanging words for people through all of history. Empires have risen and fallen, but the Bible's trustworthiness hasn't changed a bit.

We must not be people who seek to change God's Word to suit our desires. We must never ask the devil's question to justify our sins. We must allow God's Word to change our desires to His own.

CLASSICS: JOHN WESLEY

ENJOY GOD ABOVE ALL

All my springs are in thee.
PSALM 87:7 KJV

O trust in Him for happiness as well as for help. All the springs of happiness are in Him. Trust "in Him who giveth us all things richly to enjoy," who, of His own rich and free mercy, holds them out to us, as in His own hand, that, receiving them as His gifts and as pledges of His love, we may enjoy all that we possess.

It is His love gives a relish to all we taste—puts life and sweetness into all; while every creature leads us up to the great Creator, and all earth is a scale to heaven. He transfuses the joys that are at His own right hand into all He bestows on His thankful children, who, having fellowship with the Father and His Son Jesus Christ, enjoy Him in all and above all.

NEVER INDIFFERENT

A voice was heard from heaven. It said, "This is My much-loved Son. I am very happy with Him."

MATTHEW 3:17 NLV

Most parents like to extol their children's virtues. It's what makes some parents put bumper stickers on their cars telling other motorists all about their child's accomplishments. If you have children, you can probably relate.

God once took full advantage of the opportunity to let people know how proud He was of His Son. Jesus had come to the banks of the Jordan River to see John the Baptist. After John baptized Jesus, God spoke from heaven to say how happy He was with His Son.

God wasn't indifferent about Jesus, and He's not indifferent about you, either. He loved Jesus and He loves you too. He had given Jesus something to do, and He also has something for you to do. Jesus followed God, so you can do the very same thing.

GOD IS FAITHFUL

*"I am sending you grain, new wine and
olive oil, enough to satisfy you fully."*

JOEL 2:19 NIV

The prophet Joel is known for predicting a ruinous invasion of locusts. A desert locust swarm can contain tens of billions of hungry bugs whose appetites strip every green plant from the land and leave a trail of starvation in its wake.

Our troubles may feel like waves of swarming locusts. But in those times, it's important to remember that God is faithful. He will restore what the enemy longs to destroy—as Joel told his audience, God would repay them for the years the locusts had eaten (2:25).

The end of the story is yet to be written, but it is certain—so rejoice in your faithful Lord: "He sends you abundant showers, both autumn and spring rains, as before. The threshing floors will be filled with grain; the vats will overflow with new wine and oil" (Joel 2:23–24 NIV).

JESUS' CALL TO "GO FISHING"

*Jesus called out to them, "Come, follow me,
and I will show you how to fish for people!"*

MATTHEW 4:19 NLT

It was just another day of fishing. There were nets to repair, a boat to inspect, and fish to clean. Peter and his brother Andrew had been part of a fishing family for a long time. It's what they knew, and they didn't expect a career change anytime soon. Then they met Jesus.

God might call you away from the familiar and to something great. But He won't move you if you insist on staying put.

When Jesus called Peter and Andrew, He took something they knew well and transformed it into something completely different. Peter and Andrew could do nothing else. They left the nets behind and learned a new kind of fishing—this time for people who needed Jesus.

Don't be surprised when God gives you an opportunity to "fish" for people. When you follow Jesus closely, He'll make you ready to tell others about Him.

CLASSICS: CHARLES H. SPURGEON

NEVER GO BEFORE PROVIDENCE

And let it be, when thou hearest the sound of a going in the tops of the mulberry trees, that then thou shalt bestir thyself: for then shall the Lord go out before thee, to smite the host of the Philistines.

2 SAMUEL 5:24 KJV

My brethren, let us learn from David to take no steps without God. The last time you moved, or went into another business, or changed your situation in life, you asked God's help and then did it, and you were blessed in the doing of it. You have been up to this time a successful man; you have always sought God, but do not think that the stream of providence necessarily runs in a continuous current; remember, you may tomorrow without seeking God's advice venture upon a step which you will regret but once, and that will be until you die.

You have been wise hitherto; it may be because you have trusted in the Lord with all your heart and have not leaned to your own understanding. . . . If Providence tarries, tarry till Providence comes; never go before it.

GOD'S MEMORABLE GOODNESS

"But watch out! Be careful never to forget what you yourself have seen. Do not let these memories escape from your mind as long as you live! And be sure to pass them on to your children and grandchildren."

DEUTERONOMY 4:9 NLT

God did some incredible things for the Israelites as they left the land of their slavery and made their way to the promised land. Moses faithfully recorded these events in the Pentateuch—the first five books of the Bible—but one eyewitness account is not as powerful as a community of eyewitness testimonies. That's why he encouraged his fellow Israelites to both remember what God had done and to pass on their memories to future generations.

God has surely worked some miracles in your life as well. Salvation alone is a divine moment worth remembering and communicating. It is important to both remember and pass on what we've seen.

What do you remember? With whom will you share it?

THE PEACEMAKING GOD

*"Blessed are the peacemakers,
for they will be called children of God."*

MATTHEW 5:9 NIV

Why did Jesus say that God's family would be known as "peacemakers"? Probably because He knew something His audience didn't. Jesus recognized that fallen humanity seems to thrive in settings where division and anger win the day.

In a world filled with anger and division, God calls us men to seek and promote peace. Jesus told those who heard Him preach that God's family would be known as peacemakers.

We might define the word *peacemaker* as one who works to restore broken relationships. That is what God did for you and for everyone who follows Jesus. And He also richly blesses those who follow His example.

GOD GIVES POWER

So we keep on praying for you, asking our God to enable you to live a life worthy of his call. May he give you the power to accomplish all the good things your faith prompts you to do.

2 THESSALONIANS 1:11 NLT

In his second letter to the Thessalonian Christians, Paul wanted to correct their understanding about future things. In 1:7–10, he briefly explained what would happen *when* the Lord Jesus comes back. In 2:1–12, he described what would occur *before* Jesus' return. In 3:6–15, and in the scripture above, Paul describes what we should do *now*, in anticipation of that great event.

We can personalize Paul's teaching, turning the second sentence of the verse above into a prayer: "May God give me the power to accomplish all the good things my faith prompts me to do."

What is your faith in God leading you to do today? Whatever it is, He promises to give you the power you need to accomplish it.

CLASSICS: CHARLES H. SPURGEON

WHEN HEAVEN FAVORS

He raiseth up the poor out of the dust, and lifteth the needy out of the dunghill; that he may set him with princes, even with the princes of his people.

PSALM 113:7–8 KJV

"He raiseth up the poor from the dust, and lifteth the needy out of the dunghill." This has frequently occurred in providence. God in His arrangements singularly alters the position of men. History is not without many instances in which the uppermost have become lowest, and the lowest have been highest. Verily, "There are first that shall be last, and there are last that shall be first."

Solomon said, "I have seen servants upon horses, and princes walking in the dust"; and the same thing has been seen even in these modern times when kings have fled their thrones and men who were prowling about in poverty have mounted to imperial power. God in providence often laughs at pedigree and ancestry and stains the honor and dignity of everything in which human nature boasts itself. From the kennel to the palace is an easy ascent when heaven favors.

GOD CREATED ALL GOOD THINGS

Now the Holy Spirit tells us clearly that in the last times some will turn away from the true faith; they will follow deceptive spirits and teachings that come from demons. These people are hypocrites and liars, and their consciences are dead. They will say it is wrong to be married and wrong to eat certain foods. But God created those foods to be eaten with thanks by faithful people who know the truth. Since everything God created is good, we should not reject any of it but receive it with thanks.

1 TIMOTHY 4:1–4 NLT

In today's scripture, the apostle Paul speaks prophetically of the "last times," a phrase which describes a period between Jesus Christ's ascension some two thousand years ago and His return at some future point. False teachers—in Paul's time and today—create extrabiblical rules that have nothing to do with true faith, saying things like, "It is wrong to be married and wrong to eat certain foods." No! In truth, "everything God created is good." That's why we say grace before meals—thanking God for the bread, meat, vegetables, beverage. . .and dessert.

GOD'S LOVING RESPONSE

I say unto you, Love your enemies, bless them that curse you, do good to them that hate you, and pray for them which despitefully use you, and persecute you.

MATTHEW 5:44 KJV

God commands us men to love, which means there's no place for hatred, revenge, or bitterness. That is the point of today's scripture. Jesus says that when people treat you like an enemy, treat them as a friend. When they curse you, speak well of them. When they hate you, show your love by doing something good for them. When they use you, treat them better than they have treated you.

This command came from personal experience. God had experienced the hatred and curses of people He loves, yet He still offered rescue. He is treated as an enemy, yet He offers friendship. People persecuted His Son, yet He still freely offers salvation.

God has seen firsthand that His love and kindness change the way people respond to Him. Do what He does and love others—even the most unlovable.

THE LOOK OF GOD'S MERCY

For the Lord your God is a merciful God; he will not abandon or destroy you or forget the covenant with your ancestors, which he confirmed to them by oath.

DEUTERONOMY 4:31 NIV

Since God has the power and authority to punish those who break His rules, it is up to Him alone how He wants to deal with rulebreakers. Fortunately for us, God is a merciful God. But what does that mean?

Mercy is not simply the cancellation of a debt incurred by sin. It is the act of God paying that debt from His own pocket. Consider how God, who was wronged by the sin you've committed, paid the cost to correct that sin: He sent His only Son to die on the cross. What incredible mercy!

When you experience that mercy, you must then show the same to others. If you've been wronged, what would it look like to pay the debt yourself, completely forgiving the person who wronged you? It would look like God.

CLASSICS: ANDREW MURRAY

THAT SAME OMNIPOTENCE WORKS FOR US

And God said unto him, I am God Almighty: be fruitful and multiply; a nation and a company of nations shall be of thee, and kings shall come out of thy loins.

GENESIS 35:11 KJV

When God said to Abraham, "I am God Almighty," He invited him to trust His omnipotence to fulfill His promise. When Jesus went down into the grave and its impotence, it was in the faith that God's omnipotence could lift Him to the throne of His glory. It is that same Omnipotence that waits to work out God's purpose in them that believe in Him to do so. Let our hearts say, "Unto Him that is able to do exceeding abundantly above all that we ask or think, unto Him be the glory." Amen.

GOD'S GRACE IN OUR WORK

*And because the gracious hand of my God was
on me, the king granted my requests.*

NEHEMIAH 2:8 NIV

As Christians, we are saved *by* grace, *to* good works. According to the apostle Paul, "We are God's handiwork, created in Christ Jesus to do good works, which God prepared in advance for us to do" (Ephesians 2:10 NIV).

The Old Testament character Nehemiah exemplifies this truth. As an exiled Jew serving King Artaxerxes of Persia, Nehemiah learned of the broken walls of Jerusalem and longed to help out. His ultimate success in rebuilding those walls is stunning, but notice how he credits God for the first step in the process: "Because the gracious hand of my God was on me, the king granted my requests"—requests for time off, letters of safe conduct, and timber for the repairs.

Anything we need to accomplish can be done through the gracious hand of our God. He can even move the hearts of unbelievers to join in the effort. When you're performing God's will, you're unstoppable.

THE HOLY SPIRIT

"I will pour out my Spirit on all people. Your sons and daughters will prophesy, your old men will dream dreams, your young men will see visions. Even on my servants, both men and women, I will pour out my Spirit in those days. I will show wonders in the heavens and on the earth."

JOEL 2:28–30 NIV

If you're familiar with the New Testament, you probably know that the second chapter of Acts recounts the day when God fulfilled the promise of today's scripture. The promise was repeated by Jesus, namely that God would send His Holy Spirit—the third person of the Trinity—to earth to take up residence within everyone who followed Jesus.

So how important is the Holy Spirit to us today?

In Old Testament days, the Holy Spirit filled certain people at certain times to fulfill certain duties. But since what is now called Pentecost, the Holy Spirit lives within each of us, giving us the ability to live as God wants us to live, helping us to understand the scriptures, and enabling us to share our faith with others. In other words, the Holy Spirit is absolutely essential!

THE MERCIFUL GOD

And God saw their works, that they turned from their evil way; and God repented of the evil, that he had said that he would do unto them; and he did it not.

JONAH 3:10 KJV

When Jonah heard God's command to preach in Nineveh, he was dumbfounded. How could such an evil, godless city, he wondered, be worth his time? Even when the Ninevites repented, Jonah was angry, preferring that God wipe them out with His judgment.

If the Lord's mercy toward Nineveh is a testament to His eagerness to forgive, Jonah's reaction is a cautionary tale for those who do not share this mercy. Our world is full of extremely unrighteous people, but we must never forget that Jesus died for *everyone*, not just the "mostly good." We dare not view anyone as somehow less valuable than ourselves.

May we stop seeing people through the lens of their past and start considering their potential future. Then we'll come one step closer to comprehending the love God showed toward us while *we* were still sinners.

CLASSICS: CHARLES H. SPURGEON

GOD IS POWERFUL AND MERCIFUL

He healeth the broken in heart, and bindeth up their wounds.

PSALM 147:3 KJV

The next verse finely declares the power of God. "He telleth the number of the stars; he calleth them by their names." Perhaps there is nothing which gives us a nobler view of the greatness of God than a contemplation of the starry heavens. When by night we lift up our eyes and behold Him who hath created all these things. . .then indeed we adore a mighty God, and our soul naturally falls prostrate in reverential awe before the throne of Him who leads the host of heaven and marshals the stars in their armies.

But the psalmist has here placed another fact side by side with this wondrous act of God; he declares that the same God who leadeth the stars, who telleth the number of them and calleth them by their names, healeth the broken in heart and bindeth up their wounds.

GOD SEES. . .AND REWARDS

*"Your giving should be in secret. Then your
Father Who sees in secret will reward you."*

MATTHEW 6:4 NLV

Though most of us don't want to admit it, we men often struggle with insecurity—and that's why we want people to notice when we do something worth remembering. We want to be honored when we do good for others, so it hurts when we put effort into helping others but no one says a word.

God, however, wants us to feel so accepted and loved by Him that human recognition for the good we do just doesn't mean as much to us. In today's scripture, Jesus told His followers how that should work. Give, He said, and don't make a big deal about it. No one needs to know besides you—and God, who is aware of your generosity and will one day reward you.

Obey without a camera, give without a crowd, pray without a performance. There is a God who sees all, knows your heart, and is honored to find you doing the right thing—even when no one is looking.

THE WONDER OF GOD'S SOVEREIGNTY

God [is] the blessed and only Ruler,
the King of kings and Lord of lords.

1 TIMOTHY 6:15 NIV

The word *sovereign* appears nearly three hundred times in the New International Version of scripture and is embedded some sixty-seven hundred more times in the sacred divine name YHWH. The latter typically appears as the word "Lord" (with this capitalization) in most modern Bible translations.

When we think about the sovereignty of God, we begin by describing Him as all-powerful (omnipotent) and everywhere-present (omnipresent). The biblical heroes of the faith rejoiced in both aspects of God's sovereignty, and the early Christians prayed, "Sovereign Lord, you made the heavens and the earth and the sea, and everything in them" (Acts 4:24 NIV). Later, the apostle Paul described God as you see in today's scripture.

Does God's power and presence permeate every moment and millimeter of your life? Yes! You're never alone, and you're never without His power. He's asking, "What do you want Me to do for you?"

GOD'S EXCEPTIONAL HARVEST

He said to his disciples, "The harvest is great, but the workers are few. So pray to the Lord who is in charge of the harvest; ask him to send more workers into his fields."

MATTHEW 9:37–38 NLT

Jesus described God's work of rescuing workers as a "harvest." The crop is impressive, He said, but there aren't enough workers to do the work. Jesus went on to say that God is in charge of the harvest and that His followers should pray that more Christians would be willing to put feet to their faith.

Christians should encourage Christians to change the statistic from few workers to many. One good way is to pray for this. An answer to this kind of prayer means that more Christians are transformed, more people hear the good news. . .and that God's spiritual family grows larger.

These are all exceptional goals, so pray this kind of prayer. It may be that God can use you as one of His workers in His harvest.

CLASSICS: ANDREW MURRAY

IN THE LIGHT OF GOD'S HOLINESS

*But the Lord of hosts shall be exalted in judgment, and
God that is holy shall be sanctified in righteousness.*

ISAIAH 5:16 KJV

Because we are sinners and the revelation of God's holiness is in a world of sin, it is natural, it is right and meet, that the first, that the abiding impression of God's holiness should be that of an Infinite Purity that cannot look upon sin, in whose Presence it becomes the sinner to hide his face and tremble. The righteousness of God, forbidding and condemning and punishing sin, has its root in His holiness, is one of its two elements—the devouring and destroying power of the consuming fire. "God the Holy One is sanctified in righteousness"; in righteousness the holiness of the Holy One is maintained and revealed. But Light not only discovers what is impure, that it may be purified, but is in itself a thing of infinite beauty.

GOD GIVES THE WORDS

"Do not worry about what to say or how to say it. At that time you will be given what to say, for it will not be you speaking, but the Spirit of your Father."

MATTHEW 10:19–20 NIV

If someone were to ask you to tell them more about Jesus, would you feel comfortable answering the questions? Some Christians don't talk to others about the Lord much because they're afraid they'll say something wrong or look foolish. You might love God and rarely talk about Him with other people.

People have been anxious about sharing their faith for a very long time, but Jesus promised help for those who want to speak up at the moment of truth. They didn't need to worry about what to say, He said, because God would help them.

People need to hear the Gospel message, so it's important to spend time with Jesus and learn what He wants others to hear. And, at just the right moment, God will help you remember what you've learned so that you can share what you know.

GOD IS BETTER THAN EARTHLY RICHES

Command those who are rich in this present world not to be arrogant nor to put their hope in wealth, which is so uncertain, but to put their hope in God, who richly provides us with everything for our enjoyment.

1 TIMOTHY 6:17 NIV

God has much to say in His written Word about money and the place it should have in the lives of His people. Jesus Himself once said that our quest for earthly riches should never rule us, for "No one can serve two masters. Either you will hate the one and love the other, or you will be devoted to the one and despise the other. You cannot serve both God and money" (Matthew 6:24 NIV).

God doesn't want anything but Himself to capture our attention and affections. He certainly doesn't want money or earthly possessions to pull us away from Himself. When you stop and really think about it, you shouldn't either. That's because He's better—eternally and infinitely better—than anything this world has to offer.

OUR PERFECT TEACHER

*Take my yoke upon you, and learn of me; for I am meek
and lowly in heart: and ye shall find rest unto your souls.*

MATTHEW 11:29 KJV

You might sometimes think you are alone in attempting to learn everything you need to know about God. But today's scripture tells us that God won't leave you alone to figure things out for yourself. Instead, you can learn from Jesus, the perfect teacher.

Jesus' instructions are personal. He's patient, kind, and humble. And He wants you to walk with Him in a divine instructional adventure. As you do, He'll work with you as you seek to understand His ways and His teaching.

Learn from Jesus, walk with Him, and discover contentment and rest for your soul. He's your companion and your teacher, and He wants you to learn more and more about Him each day.

CLASSICS: ANDREW MURRAY

SING PRAISE TO OUR HOLY GOD

And in that day shall ye say, Praise the Lord, call upon his name, declare his doings among the people, make mention that his name is exalted. Sing unto the Lord; for he hath done excellent things: this is known in all the earth. Cry out and shout, thou inhabitant of Zion: for great is the Holy One of Israel in the midst of thee.

ISAIAH 12:4–6 KJV

As it is in the redemption of His people that God's holiness is revealed, so it is in the song of redemption that the personal ascription of holiness to God is found. We know how in scripture, after some striking special interposition of God as Redeemer, the special influence of the Spirit is manifested in some song of praise. It is remarkable how it is in these outbursts of holy enthusiasm, God is praised as the Holy One. See it in the song of Hannah (1 Samuel 2:2), "There is none holy as the Lord." The language of the Seraphim (Isaiah 6) is that of a song of adoration. In the great day of Israel's deliverance the song will be, "The Lord Jehovah is become my strength and song. Sing unto the Lord, for He hath done excellent things. Cry aloud and shout, thou inhabitant of Zion, for great is *the Holy One* of Israel in the midst of thee."

DO GOOD EVERY DAY

Then [Jesus] turned to his critics and asked, "Does the law permit good deeds on the Sabbath, or is it a day for doing evil? Is this a day to save life or to destroy it?"

MARK 3:4 NLT

As Jesus entered a synagogue one Sabbath day, He met a man with a withered hand. Jesus knew two things: that this man needed help. . .and that a group of Jewish religious leaders was watching Him closely.

Jesus knew what these men were thinking, so He turned their yet-unasked questions around on them. "Does the law permit good deeds on the Sabbath?" He asked.

These self-righteous religious leaders didn't catch Jesus' point, but we should today. God wants us to love our neighbors, and there is never a wrong day to put action behind that love.

When you have an opportunity to love your neighbor on your own day of rest—say, by stopping on your way to church and helping someone change a flat on a rainy day—do it! You'll bless others, and you'll glorify the God who wants you to do good for others every day.

GOD'S FAVORITE SONG

"[He] will rejoice over you with singing."
ZEPHANIAH 3:17 NIV

For believers, worshipping God in music and song should be one of the most significant events in life. Worship is singing songs of thanks and praising God for all the good things He has done.

That should be pretty obvious. But did you know that God rejoices over you in the same way?

We know our shortcomings all too well. Maybe that's why it can be so hard to believe our Lord really does love us deeply, completely, even passionately. *Passion* is a strong word, and it tends to lead to strong action. What are you passionate about?

The Bible says God's passion is *you*. In fact, He loves you so much He's singing over you right now. Why not take a little time and try to listen for His voice today?

GOD ALONE

"Has any nation ever heard the voice of God speaking from fire—as you did—and survived? Has any other god dared to take a nation for himself out of another nation by means of trials, miraculous signs, wonders, war, a strong hand, a powerful arm, and terrifying acts? Yet that is what the Lord your God did for you in Egypt, right before your eyes. He showed you these things so you would know that the Lord is God and there is no other."

DEUTERONOMY 4:33–35 NLT

For the Israelites who exited Egypt, there was no excuse for denying God's existence or power. They encountered His greatness firsthand. Then they did what humans do and forgot the miracles whenever new fears popped up. In their fear, they'd make new gods and hope for the best.

God is real not just to those who have seen His wonders but to everyone. We may not fashion idols today, but our fears often tell us to chase solutions other than God's provision.

This must not be! The Lord is God and there is no other.

GOD LOVES TO MAKE HOLY

The meek also shall increase their joy in the LORD, and the poor among men shall rejoice in the Holy One of Israel.

ISAIAH 29:19 KJV

In Paradise we saw that God the Creator was God the Sanctifier, perfecting the work of His hands. In Israel we saw that God the Redeemer was ever God the Sanctifier, making holy the people He had chosen for Himself. Here in Isaiah we see how it is God the Sanctifier, the Holy One, who is to bring about the great redemption of the New Testament: as the Holy One, He is the Redeemer.

God redeems because He is holy and loves to make holy: Holiness will be redemption perfected. Redemption and holiness together are to be found in the personal relation to God. The key to the secret of holiness is offered to each believer in that word: "Thus saith the Lord, your Redeemer, the Holy One of Israel: I am the Lord, your Holy One." To come more to know, to possess the Holy One and be possessed of Him is holiness.

NATURE'S CONDUCTOR

*When Jesus woke up, he rebuked the wind and
said to the waves, "Silence! Be still!" Suddenly
the wind stopped, and there was a great calm.*

MARK 4:39 NLT

Doing what God commands seems tough for humans,
but nature doesn't have that problem. At His command,
seasons follow each other, rain and snow fall, the sun
rises and sets—even the wind and waves obey Him.

If nature is a symphony, then God is the Conductor.
Each part of nature follows His direction. The seas
move and sway according to His pleasure. He brings
bears out of hibernation and directs salmon to swim
upstream to reproduce.

This is the God of creation, who invites you to
marvel at the natural wonders around you—and love
Him. If you find joy at the sight of a canyon in summer
or a mountain in winter, remember that these things
are His gift to you. Enjoy them.

JESUS' UNSHAKABLE FAITHFULNESS

*If we are faithless, he [Jesus Christ] remains
faithful, for he cannot disown himself.*

2 TIMOTHY 2:13 NIV

What is it that we have to do before dying? The apostle Paul tells us in his very last epistle: no matter what, remain faithful!

In 2 Timothy 1:3–2:13, Paul encourages Timothy—and other believers, including you and me—to be faithful to the Lord in all times and circumstances. In turn, our faithfulness is a matter of stirring up the gift of God within us, never being ashamed of those who suffer for the Lord's sake, dedicating ourselves to holy living, keeping a good grip on the Christian faith imparted to us, working long and hard to do the Lord's will, and enduring whatever suffering comes our way.

Then Paul concludes with today's scripture. How good that our Lord Jesus always remains faithful. Know that He empowers us to do the same.

GOD GIVES GENEROUSLY

Elijah said, "Go and tell Ahab, 'Hitch up your chariot and go down before the rain stops you.'"

1 KINGS 18:44 NIV

You probably know the story of Elijah's triumph over the prophets of Baal. But did you realize it's bookended by the story of a drought?

In 1 Kings 17:1 (NIV), Elijah tells the evil King Ahab, "As the LORD, the God of Israel, lives, whom I serve, there will be neither dew nor rain in the next few years except at my word." (NIV). After his incredible victory on Mount Carmel, Elijah told Ahab the rain was coming. In fact, the king should get moving since the rain would be heavy enough to stop him.

That's the way God gives. Whether in physical, emotional, or spiritual terms, He has resources we can't even imagine. . .and He gives to His children generously, wisely, and at the perfect moment. Ask for His help, and stay faithful.

CLASSICS: CHARLES H. SPURGEON

CONFESSING TO THE OMNISCIENT GOD

Lord, all my desire is before thee;
and my groaning is not hid from thee.

PSALM 38:9 KJV

It may be said that God knows our desires and that this is what the text itself asserts. I do not doubt the omniscience of God; but He bids us confess everything to Him quite as carefully as if He did not know it until we informed Him. We are to tell out our cases for ourselves just as David did, for it was not until after he had told out his sad story in the eight previous verses that he said, "All my desire is before thee."

We may expect the Lord to treat us as if He did not know our desires if we are negligent in declaring them. Does not the apostle say, "In everything by prayer and supplication with thanksgiving let your requests be made known unto God"?

THE FAIR JUDGE

The soul that sinneth, it shall die. The son shall not bear the iniquity of the father, neither shall the father bear the iniquity of the son.

EZEKIEL 18:20 KJV

One of God's attributes emphasized throughout the Bible—and that lies at the core of Jesus' crucifixion—is His fairness. Human laws have varied throughout history, but God's judgments and rewards are consistent at every time and every place.

Long before the Holy Spirit began dwelling in believers' bodies, God emphasized the personal aspect of humanity's relationship to Him. Each individual had the responsibility of deciding whether or not to obey God's laws, and God gave a fair judgment based upon that choice alone. Bloodlines didn't matter.

Now that Jesus' sacrifice has torn the veil between us and God, the relevance of this truth has only amplified. Never label your upbringing as the reason for your spiritual condition. Your parents may or may not have followed God, but the important question is this: Do *you*?

AN AMAZING TEACHER

When the Sabbath came, [Jesus] began to teach in the synagogue, and many who heard him were amazed.

MARK 6:2 NIV

If you want to hear some amazing teaching, pay attention to Jesus. His words fill the Gospels of Matthew, Mark, Luke, and John. And in the verse above, you can see the response of those who heard Him teach: amazement.

Jesus' teaching in Mark 6:1–6 took place in His hometown synagogue—a Jewish house of worship, similar to a church today. The people who heard Him were used to religious conversations, and they knew the Old Testament. They knew God had a plan to bring the long-awaited Messiah into their midst. They knew facts, stories, and the right words to say. Yet Jesus' words that day were different from any they had ever heard.

Jesus was the greatest teacher of all time. His teachings can be found in the New Testament, and they can encourage you, challenge you, instruct you, comfort you, and *amaze* you—today and every day.

THE MYSTERY OF GOD

Hear, O Israel: The LORD our God, the LORD is one.
DEUTERONOMY 6:4 NIV

God is the triune deity—the Three-in-One. This is one of the great mysteries of God. How can God be Father, Son, and Spirit, each unique in role and function, each still fully God, connected seamlessly as the great I AM?

Theologians and writers have tried in vain to capture this mystery in metaphor, but who God is cannot be entirely pinned down by definitions. If we fully understood the mystery, we would have fewer reasons for faith. The mystery of God's triune nature is one to be embraced and celebrated as true without needing to break it down.

God invites us into the mystery not to give us answers but to simply enjoy His presence. So spend a few minutes in prayer today. Talk to God the Father because of what the Son did on the cross, sending His Spirit to dwell inside you. Engage with the mystery.

CLASSICS: D. L. MOODY

GOD STRENGTHENS US

Fear thou not; for I am with thee: be not dismayed; for I am thy God: I will strengthen thee; yea, I will help thee; yea, I will uphold thee with the right hand of my righteousness.

ISAIAH 41:10 KJV

Christ is our Keeper. A great many young disciples are afraid they will not hold out. "He that keepeth Israel shall neither slumber nor sleep" (Psalm 121:4). It is the work of Christ to keep us; and if He keeps us there will be no danger of our falling. . . .

We are no match for Satan; he has had six thousand years' experience. But then we remember that the One who neither slumbers nor sleeps is our keeper. We read, "Fear thou not, for I am with thee; be not dismayed, for I am thy God; I will strengthen thee; yea, I will help thee; yea, I will uphold thee with the right hand of My righteousness."

GOD'S WRITTEN WORD

All Scripture is God-breathed and is useful for teaching, rebuking, correcting and training in righteousness, so that the servant of God may be thoroughly equipped for every good work.

2 TIMOTHY 3:16–17 NIV

As a former Jewish religious leader, the apostle Paul was deeply, intimately familiar with God's written Word. In Paul's day, the complete Bible hadn't yet been compiled, but he knew how important scripture (what we now call the Old Testament) is in the life of the Christian.

God gave us Christians the entire Bible—Old and New Testament alike—to reveal Himself to us. His Word shows us who He is, what He wants from us, and how we can have a deeply personal, mutually loving relationship with our Creator.

Do you want to know God more intimately and learn what He truly desires from and for you? Then read, study, and memorize His Word!

FLEEING FROM GOD?

The word of the Lord came to Jonah son of Amittai: "Go to the great city of Nineveh and preach against it, because its wickedness has come up before me." But Jonah ran away from the Lord.

JONAH 1:1–3 NIV

In Psalm 139, David reflected on the greatness of God and the intimate relationship He had with His created beings. David asked, rhetorically, "Where can I go from your Spirit? Where can I flee from your presence?" (verse 7 NIV). The answer, of course, is that David couldn't possibly hide or flee from God, even if he wanted to.

Trying to flee from the Lord is never a good idea, even it were possible. The prophet Jonah learned that lesson the hard way. He had his reasons for wanting to avoid God's call—to go to Nineveh and preach to the wicked people living there. So he ran the opposite direction.

God let Jonah run but ultimately got his attention. Whatever the Lord is calling you to do today, just do it. There's no fleeing from Him. But why would you want to?

RELATIONSHIP NOT RELIGION

"You put away the Laws of God and obey the laws made by men."
MARK 7:8 NLV

The verse above shows a contrast between religion and a real relationship with God. During Jesus' earthly ministry, some religious people chose notoriety instead of new life. They sought to be seen as honorable instead of honoring God from their hearts. Others, however, chose to follow God personally. They followed Him imperfectly, but they followed—and that made all the difference.

Following manmade laws can make us appear to be following and loving God, but He has a far better way: walking in a close, authentic relationship with Him as our loving heavenly Father and us as His beloved children.

Following God is about the relationship that grows between Him and us. It's a gift of love and forgiveness, and it's far more satisfying to our souls.

CLASSICS: D. L. MOODY

HONOR GOD, AND HE WILL HONOR YOU

When thou passest through the waters, I will be with thee; and through the rivers, they shall not overflow thee: when thou walkest through the fire, thou shalt not be burned; neither shall the flame kindle upon thee.

ISAIAH 43:2 KJV

God can take care of us when we pass through the waters; God can take care of us when we pass through the fires. . . . God will take care of us, if we will but stand up for Him.

Young man, honor God; and God will honor you. What you have to do is to take your stand upon God's side. And if you have to go against the whole world, take that stand. Dare to do right; dare to be true; dare to be honest: let the consequences be what they may. You may have to forfeit your situation; because you cannot, and will not, do something your employer requires you to do, but which your conscience tells you is wrong. Give up your situation then, rather than give up your principles.

JESUS IS THE MESSIAH

[Jesus] asked them, "But who do you say I am?"
Peter replied, "You are the Messiah."

MARK 8:29 NLT

Peter was the impulsive disciple whose faulty choices are legendary. He promised to stay and then ran away. He said Jesus was worth dying for and then denied he knew the Lord. He said he had faith and then he doubted. This was Peter—and Jesus loved him.

Peter was the first disciple to acknowledge that Jesus was the Messiah, the One God had promised would come and deliver freedom. The disciples hoped, prayed, and longed for the Messiah, but who told them He had arrived? Peter.

Many believe that Jesus was a good man, a great leader, and an inspirational teacher, but the truth that He is the Savior, Redeemer, and Rescuer escapes most people. Jesus came to rescue sinners from eternal judgment by dying a sacrificial death and being raised from the dead. Because Jesus, God in the flesh, did that, we can live with Him through all eternity. Just ask.

GOD IS LOVE

And thou shalt love the Lord thy God with all thine heart, and with all thy soul, and with all thy might.

DEUTERONOMY 6:5 KJV

We treat people we love differently. We listen when they speak, praise them when they impress us, and enjoy being in their presence just because of who they are. When this love is returned, it spills outward into other relationships. We treat acquaintances better than we otherwise would because we do not seek love from them; we have more than enough and must share it.

The commandment from today's verse is not only a requirement for our relationship with God. It is the inevitable result from the love that God places within us. John stated this truth well when he wrote, "And we have known and believed the love that God hath to us. God is love; and he that dwelleth in love dwelleth in God, and God in him. . . . We love him, because he first loved us" (1 John 4:16, 19 KJV).

GOD INCLUDES; SO SHOULD WE

"Whoever welcomes one of these little children in my name welcomes me; and whoever welcomes me does not welcome me but the one who sent me."

MARK 9:37 NIV

One of the most inclusive messages ever expressed is that God is willing to accept anyone. He loves everyone. The scripture above points this out in a different way. When you pay attention to children, love them, care for them, and help them learn, you are paying attention to Jesus and His Father.

Jesus seemed to link the idea of compassion for others as a way to become more connected with God. It was as if He was saying you can't really love God if you have no ability to love the people He created.

Christ followers will care about the struggles of others. . .won't reject some people while accepting others. . .will want the best for all. This is the kind of love God has for you—and the kind of love He wants you to give away.

CLASSICS: D. L. MOODY

GREATER THAN CAESAR, NAPOLEON, OR ALEXANDER

Now therefore send, and gather to me all Israel unto mount Carmel, and the prophets of Baal four hundred and fifty, and the prophets of the groves four hundred, which eat at Jezebel's table.

1 KINGS 18:19 KJV

When Elijah stood on Mount Carmel, Ahab did not see who was with him. Little did he know the prophet's God; little did he think that, when Elijah walked up Mount Carmel, God walked with him. Talk of an Alexander making the world tremble at the tread of his armies! Of the marches and victories of a Caesar, or a Napoleon! The man who is walking with God is greater than all the Caesars and Napoleons and Alexanders who ever lived. Little did Ahab and the false prophets of Baal know that Elijah was walking with the same God with whom Enoch walked before the flood. Elijah was nothing when out of communion with God; but when walking in the power of God, he stood on Mount Carmel like a king.

A RIGHTEOUS JUDGE

I have fought the good fight, I have finished the race, and I have remained faithful. And now the prize awaits me—the crown of righteousness, which the Lord, the righteous Judge, will give me on the day of his return. And the prize is not just for me but for all who eagerly look forward to his appearing.

2 TIMOTHY 4:7–8 NLT

The last chapter of 2 Timothy contains the final recorded words of Paul before his martyrdom in Rome. In 4:1–18, Paul tells Timothy "I have remained faithful" (as you see above) and charges the younger man to do the same.

Our success is a matter of living with eternity in view, for we have a righteous Judge who will one day reward us according to our faithfulness to Him in this life. God loves us and longs to reward our dedication to scripture, our persistence, our patience, our right thinking, our willingness to suffer, and our commitment to ministry even near the end of our lives on earth.

Paul's stellar example—and Jesus Christ's stirring words, "Be thou faithful unto death" (Revelation 2:10 KJV)—should challenge every Christian man even today.

AN INCOMPARABLY GOOD GOD

*Jesus said to him, "Why do you call Me good?
There is only One Who is good. That is God."*

MARK 10:18 NLV

A rich man approached Jesus, asking what he needed to do to reach heaven. This man was certain he qualified—he knew the rules and followed them faithfully. He considered himself blessed because he was rich. If Jesus could just certify his place in heaven, he'd have one more thing to brag about. But Jesus took this questioner to a different place.

The Son of God asked why this rich man called Him "good." That was a term belonging to God alone. Perhaps Jesus was leading the man to an important realization—that Jesus was not just a great teacher and miracle worker but also God in the flesh and therefore worthy of being called "good."

Jesus' question to the rich man should lead us to a simple, wonderful truth: God *is* good—incomparably good in every way.

JESUS PAID OUR DEBT

So if you consider me a partner, welcome [Onesimus] as you would welcome me. If he has done you any wrong or owes you anything, charge it to me.

PHILEMON 17–18 NIV

Philemon is the first New Testament "postcard epistle," the really short ones that include 2 and 3 John and Jude. In the end, it's all about love—the kind of love that compels one man to reach out and advocate for another man in serious trouble—even offering to pay a debt that man could never pay on his own.

Paul never stopped marveling at the way God demonstrated His love for us by giving His Son, who then gave His life on our behalf and now advocates for us before a holy God. And Paul followed Jesus' example by advocating for a runaway slave named Onesimus—even offering to pay any debts he had incurred to his master, Philemon.

What a friend Paul proved to be to Onesimus. And what a friend Jesus is to us!

CLASSICS: JOHN WESLEY

GOD IS EVERYWHERE— YOU ARE NEVER ALONE

Am I a God at hand, saith the Lord, and not a God afar off?
Can any hide himself in secret places that I shall not see him?
saith the Lord. Do not I fill heaven and earth? saith the Lord.

JEREMIAH 23:23–24 KJV

How strongly and beautifully do these words express
the omnipresence of God! And can there be in the
whole compass of nature a more sublime subject? Can
there be any more worthy the consideration of every
rational creature? Is there any more necessary to be
considered and to be understood so far as our poor
faculties will admit? How many excellent purposes
may it answer! What deep instruction may it convey
to all the children of men! And more directly to the
children of God.

"BUT GOD WILL"

Pharaoh said to Joseph, "I had a dream, and no one can interpret it. But I have heard it said of you that when you hear a dream you can interpret it." "I cannot do it," Joseph replied to Pharaoh, "but God will give Pharaoh the answer he desires."

GENESIS 41:15–16 NIV

Even the most powerful men run up against forces they can't control. So what can we say for the average guy who struggles just to pay bills or keep his kids on the straight and narrow path?

Actually, the realization of our own powerlessness is the first step toward accessing the unlimited power of God. Consider the Old Testament hero Joseph, who accomplished incredible things because the Lord was with him (Genesis 39:2). He caught the attention of the Egyptian pharaoh, the most powerful man on earth, who'd had a pair of strange and troubling dreams. "I hear that you can explain them," Pharaoh basically said to Joseph. "No, not me," Joseph replied. "But God will."

When crunch time comes—when we recognize our utter inability to accomplish the vital task—God steps in. And He always does things right.

A GOD WHO DISCIPLINES

Now the Lord provided a huge fish to swallow Jonah, and Jonah was in the belly of the fish three days and three nights.

JONAH 1:17 NIV

The Bible teaches that God disciplines those He loves—and that the discipline is sometimes harsh. (Think of the rebellious people of Judah being carted away to Babylon.) The writer of Hebrews 12:6 (NIV) put it like this: "The Lord disciplines the one he loves, and he chastens everyone he accepts as his son."

God loved Jonah, so when the prophet tried to run, there was some very unpleasant discipline. Jonah was sent to a three-day stay in what must have been as foul as anything we can imagine.

While in the belly of that great fish, Jonah had some come-to-the-Lord time. He ended up praising God and agreeing to do what he'd been asked to do in the first place.

Obedience is always our best choice. But when we mess up and feel God's hand of discipline, let's recognize that for what it truly is: love.

THE GOD WHO FORGIVES

"Come, let us return to the Lord. He has torn us to pieces; now he will heal us. He has injured us; now he will bandage our wounds."

HOSEA 6:1 NLT

The Israelites had a bumpy relationship with their Creator: every time they emerged from their wickedness and began following God, they almost immediately turned on their heels and plunged back into sin.

God was understandably furious with them each time. He'd rescued them from slavery, parting an ocean along the way, and sent countless prophets to lead them in the right direction. . .and still they disobeyed.

But God kept forgiving them. In fact, Hosea wrote that God was waiting to heal His people, even after He'd just finished punishing them for their disobedience!

As Jesus instructed His disciples to forgive their enemies until "seventy times seven" (Matthew 18:22 KJV), He undoubtedly thought of the unfathomable forgiveness God had shown toward the Israelites. Once we consider the depths of God's mercy, the petty wrongs we receive at the hands of others will become easier for us to forgive as well.

CLASSICS: CHARLES H. SPURGEON

WORSHIP GOD ALONE

[Hezekiah] removed the high places, and brake the images, and cut down the groves, and brake in pieces the brasen serpent that Moses had made: for unto those days the children of Israel did burn incense to it: and he called it Nehushtan.

2 KINGS 18:4 KJV

The first commandment instructs us that there is but one God, who alone is to be worshipped; and the second commandment teaches that no attempt is to be made to represent the Lord, neither are we to bow down before any form of sacred similitude. . . . The two commandments thus make a full sweep of idolatry. We are not to worship any other god; we are not to worship the true God by the use of representative symbols. He is a Spirit and is to be worshipped in spirit and in truth, and not by the use of visible imagery. . . .

To Jesus must all adoring eyes be turned, and to the Holy Spirit the revealer of the truth, and to our Father who is in heaven; and we must receive the Gospel not as the word of man, but as it is in truth, the Word of God. Love the ministers of Christ, but fall not into that form of brazen serpent worship which will degrade you into the servants of men.

A GOD WITH A PLAN

*Mary responded, "Oh, how my soul praises the Lord.
How my spirit rejoices in God my Savior!"*

LUKE 1:46–47 NLT

Today's scripture is one person's reaction to God's plan for bringing the Savior into the world. This plan would carry with it good news to people around the world. In order to be a part of that plan, Mary just needed to agree with God, then do what He said. She would become the mother of Jesus! Mary hadn't expected to be instrumental in bringing the long-awaited Messiah into the world, but because she believed God, because she trusted His plan, she could praise and rejoice in Him. And she obeyed.

What's your reaction when you know what God wants you to do? When you know God's plan, is it easy to follow? Do you rejoice simply because God is good and wants to bless you and others? Be like Mary—believe and obey, then rejoice in the Lord.

THE GIVER OF GOOD THINGS

"You must recognize that the Lord your God is not giving you this good land because you are good, for you are not—you are a stubborn people."

DEUTERONOMY 9:6 NLT

God sometimes gives people what they deserve. We call this "justice." When people deserve His punishment but do not get it, we call it "mercy." When God gives good things to undeserving people, we call it "grace."

It is because of God's grace that we have good things in our lives. We may be tempted to think that we receive good things because of our hard work, our great attitudes, or our outstanding abilities. We want to be responsible for the good but hesitate to accept our share for the evil that exists in the world. We are a stubborn people.

When we realize we are the recipients of undeserved goodness, we should be more willing to bestow goodness on others, deserving or not. In so doing, we become more like God, gracious and good.

WORSHIP GOD'S SON, JESUS CHRIST

*The Son radiates God's own glory and expresses the
very character of God, and he sustains everything
by the mighty power of his command.*

HEBREWS 1:3 NLT

The Bible says Jesus Christ is the Son of God, equal with God, and fully God. Jesus is a member of what we call the Trinity: Father, Son, and Holy Spirit. The Son is infinite and eternal. He made all things, and by Him all things exist. God the Father is putting all things under Him.

Scripture also teaches that Jesus is the Savior, Deliverer, Redeemer. He died on a Roman cross—a horrific punishment reserved for the worst criminals. But Jesus was no criminal—He died to take the penalty for our sins, and not just for ours but for the sins of the whole world. Truly, He "is the Savior of the world" (John 4:42 NLT).

God's Word says Jesus is the Victor, Overcomer, Conqueror. He physically rose from the grave, having defeated sin and death. He is the King of kings and Lord of lords. . .and completely worthy of our worship.

CLASSICS: CHARLES H. SPURGEON

NO GUESSWORK WITH GOD

*O Lord, thou hast pleaded the causes of
my soul; thou hast redeemed my life.*

LAMENTATIONS 3:58 KJV

You must not fail to observe how positively he speaks. He doth not say, "I hope, I trust, I sometimes think, that God hath pleaded the causes of my soul"; but he speaks of it as a matter of fact not to be disputed. "Thou hast pleaded the causes of my soul."

Let us, brethren, by the aid of the gracious Comforter, shake off those doubts and fears which so much mar our peace and comfort. Be this our prayer today that we may have done with the harsh croaking voice of surmise and suspicion and may be able to speak with the clear, melodious voice of full assurance, "I know whom I have believed, and am persuaded that he is able to keep that which I have committed unto him."

GOD ENABLES US TO REACH THE LOST

[Jesus] continued to travel around, preaching in synagogues throughout Judea.

LUKE 4:44 NLT

Jesus came to earth with a purpose and a plan. He could have kept to Himself—observing humanity from a distance—but He gave His time, wisdom, and love instead. Even though Jesus spent most of His time ministering to those who needed Him, He also was very intentional about spending time alone with His Father in heaven. That kept Him completely connected to God—and also empowered Him to reach out to people with a special kind of love and power.

Even though Jesus was God's own Son—literally God in the flesh—He still needed to spend time with His Father in prayer. And if you want to be empowered to love others as Jesus did, you'll need to do the very same thing.

JESUS SUFFERED FOR US

Since he himself [Jesus Christ] has gone through suffering and testing, he is able to help us when we are being tested.

HEBREWS 2:18 NLT

In the hours before Jesus died on a Roman cross, He experienced more anguish and endured more pain than we can imagine. By His shed blood, Jesus saved us from our sins, gave us a new heart, granted us eternal life, and made it possible for us to be adopted into God's family forever. What incredible, eternal blessings from this ultimate sacrifice: God's Son for you and me.

By His suffering, Jesus also set an example for us. As today's scripture indicates (along with 1 Peter 2:21), we can follow the Lord through our own suffering, knowing that He will be there to help us. He is present in and uses suffering to make us more like Himself.

If, like Christ, we patiently endure suffering to the end, we'll be richly blessed and eternally rewarded by God (Romans 5:3–5, Hebrews 12:1–15, and James 1:2–12).

EVERYTHING BELONGS TO GOD

To the Lord your God belong the heavens, even the highest heavens, the earth and everything in it.

DEUTERONOMY 10:14 NIV

The richest billionaire and the penniless widow have this in common: neither of them owns a thing. Not really. Not in the long-term, definitely. Everything—and this is an important thing to realize and remember— belongs to God.

We do not own. At most, we steward. We take care of the things that belong to God, and we will answer to Him for how we have used His things.

Is there a high balance in your bank account? Great! How will you use God's money to spread truth, love, and mercy to the world? Is your bank account empty? No matter. How will you use your talents to bring people to God?

When you realize that you own nothing—because everything is God's—you'll be less likely to tighten your fists around God's resources and more likely to open your hands to help.

CLASSICS: CHARLES H. SPURGEON

ONLY ONE WAY

And when Aaron lighteth the lamps at even, he shall burn incense upon it, a perpetual incense before the Lord throughout your generations.

EXODUS 30:8 KJV

Never try to draw near to God in prayer or praise or meditation or scripture reading or holy service apart from Jesus Christ, or your attempt must be a failure. Through the wall of fire which surrounds the throne you can only pass by way of the one door, namely, the body and blood of our great Mediator, Sacrifice and Substitute. Is not that door sufficient? Why should we climb up some other way? If I am very heavy of heart, do not let me try to raise my spirits, and so come in the power of human courage; but let me come just as I am, made bold through Him whose comforts delight my soul. If I feel that I have been sinning, do not let me try to get rid of my sin by some other process and then draw near to God; but let me come, sinner as I am, in the name of the sinner's Savior, and so draw near to God, having washed my robes and made them white in the blood of the Lamb.

JESUS DOES THE HUMANLY IMPOSSIBLE

"Which is easier to say, 'Your sins are forgiven,' or, 'Get up and walk'?"

LUKE 5:23 NLV

A lame man was brought to Jesus. The man's friends had gone to extraordinary lengths to bring him to Jesus, tearing a hole in the roof of the house where Jesus was teaching and then lowering his bed so Jesus could help him.

The people already in the house, including some proud religious leaders, had no idea what would happen next. But Jesus caused gasps of outrage from the religious leaders when He said to the crippled man, "Friend, your sins are forgiven" (Luke 5:20 NLV).

Jesus had the power to heal this man, and He had the authority to declare the man's sins forgiven. Both were humanly impossible, the business of God alone. That day, though, Jesus announced that He had the ability to do what only God could do for people around Him then and for us now—because He *is* God.

GOD GIVES SECOND CHANCES

Then the word of the Lord came to Jonah a second time: "Go to the great city of Nineveh and proclaim to it the message I give you." Jonah obeyed the word of the Lord and went to Nineveh.

JONAH 3:1–3 NIV

Jonah was reluctant to go to Nineveh the first time God asked. And with good reason—at least humanly speaking.

The brutality of the Assyrians was extreme, even by ancient standards. So, when God commanded Jonah to preach against Nineveh, he knew exactly what he was getting into. That's why he fled—in the opposite direction.

Jonah's assessment of the situation faltered on one key point: he forgot to factor in the infinite power of his almighty God. When Jonah finally traveled to Nineveh and preached, the king repented and then demanded that everyone else do the same. . .and they did. All because God gave Jonah a second chance to obey.

It's never too late to do the right thing. Today can be the day that changes everything.

GOD IS ALL-EVERYTHING

Neither is there any creature that is not manifest in his sight: but all things are naked and opened unto the eyes of him with whom we have to do.

HEBREWS 4:13 KJV

When we say "God is omnipresent," it means that He is present everywhere. That sounds simple enough—until you seek ways to apply this definition to who God really is.

Is the word *omnipresent* in the Bible? No. Instead, the Word says the eyes of God see everything everywhere. Where does the Bible teach this? It's taught in Psalm 113:4–6, Psalm 139:7–10, Proverbs 15:3, Isaiah 57:15, Jeremiah 23:23–24, Zechariah 4:10, today's scripture, and many others.

What other "omni" words describe God? First, *omnipotent* means all-powerful. Second, *omniscient* means all-knowing. Taken together, these three words speak of God's absolute sovereignty over the heavens and earth. Truly, our God reigns!

CLASSICS: ANDREW MURRAY

POWER IN GOD'S NAME

So will I make my holy name known in the midst of my people Israel; and I will not let them pollute my holy name any more: and the heathen shall know that I am the LORD, the Holy One in Israel.

EZEKIEL 39:7 KJV

"*Hallowed be Thy name.*" What name? This new name of the Father. The word *holy* is the central word of the Old Testament; the name *Father* of the New. In this name of Love all the holiness and glory of God are now to be revealed.

And how is the name to be hallowed? By God Himself: "I will hallow My great name which ye have profaned." Our prayer must be that in ourselves, in all God's children, in presence of the world, God Himself would reveal the holiness, the divine power, the hidden glory of the name of Father. The Spirit of the Father is the Holy Spirit; it is only when we yield ourselves to be led of Him that the name will be hallowed in our prayers and our lives. Let us learn the prayer: "Our Father, hallowed be Thy name."

THE GOD WHO SATISFIES

"God blesses you who are hungry now, for you will be satisfied. God blesses you who weep now, for in due time you will laugh."

LUKE 6:21 NLT

It's possible that you've never faced hunger in your life. It may be that you've never wondered where or how you would get your next meal. It can be safe to assume that God makes sure His family always has enough food to eat. After all, Jesus prayed for food in the Lord's Prayer.

In today's verse, though, Jesus speaks of a different kind of hunger—a hunger that only God Himself can satisfy. You need God's presence, forgiveness, and love. . .as well as a forever home. You need His companionship, comfort, and compassion. What you hunger for in Him can't be found in a grocery store. It comes only from knowing and following Jesus with your whole heart and mind.

BEYOND OUR EXPECTATIONS

"For the LORD your God is the God of gods and Lord of lords. He is the great God, the mighty and awesome God, who shows no partiality and cannot be bribed."

DEUTERONOMY 10:17 NLT

When the Egyptians, Greeks, and Norsemen created their pantheons, they sought to explain natural phenomena with supernatural deities. The gods they made reflected their values and the capriciousness of their whims. Their gods might be tempted or assuaged with bribes, but no one knew for sure that their gods would help or love them.

God Almighty is different. He loves because He is love. He deserves praise because He is praiseworthy. He cannot be bribed because He is wholly just. And He cannot be fully understood by humans because we were made in His image, not Him in ours.

Praise God for being beyond our expectations and explanations! He is not like other gods because He is more real than reality itself.

JESUS' IMMENSE PATIENCE

*Here is a trustworthy saying that deserves full acceptance:
Christ Jesus came into the world to save sinners—of
whom I am the worst. But for that very reason I was shown
mercy so that in me, the worst of sinners, Christ Jesus
might display his immense patience as an example for
those who would believe in him and receive eternal life.*

1 TIMOTHY 1:15–16 NIV

What does the word *immense* bring to mind? A blue
whale? A snowcapped mountain? The vast expanse
of space? Would you attach it to the word *patience*?

The apostle Paul did, when he considered his history with Jesus.

As you may know, Paul was originally called Saul,
a rabidly anti-Christian Jewish leader who persecuted
Jesus' early followers to the death (Acts 22:4). That's
why, after his miraculous conversion on the road to
Damascus, Paul called himself "the worst" of sinners.

It's also why God showed mercy to Paul. If the
worst of sinners could find grace, then who *couldn't*?
Jesus felt that persecution as if it were being done to
Himself (Acts 9:4), but still showed immense patience
to Paul. He shows that same patience to each and
every one of us.

CLASSICS: ANDREW MURRAY

GOD IN YOU

Now let them put away their whoredom, and the carcases of their kings, far from me, and I will dwell in the midst of them for ever.

EZEKIEL 43:9 KJV

The question, How is God going to be my God? finds its answer in the words: "God hath said, I will dwell in them, and I will be their God." That is God's answer to your question. And what a wonderful answer it is. . . .

How little we think that our heart was actually created that God might dwell there, that He might show forth His life and love there, and that there our love and joy might be in Him alone. How little we know that just as naturally as we have the love of parents or children filling our heart and making us happy, we can have the living God, for whom the heart was made, dwelling there and filling it with His own goodness and blessedness. This is my message this evening: God wants your heart; if you give it Him, He will dwell in it.

THE IMPENETRABLE FORTRESS

*The LORD is good, a strong hold in the day of trouble;
and he knoweth them that trust in him.*

NAHUM 1:7 KJV

Israel was a nation at war. While it had moments of peace, many surrounding nations constantly sought to disrupt that peace, and the Old Testament chronicles the countless battles that resulted.

Therefore, Nahum's description of God as a "strong hold" would have resonated deeply with his readers. God was not just on their side—He was their sole refuge. When the fighting became too intense, only He could give them peace and strength.

Not much has changed. We as Christians are still waging war against a powerful enemy. . .but this time our foe is far more dangerous. He has traded arrows for fiery darts and chariots for subtlety. Our only hope against such an infernal adversary rests in the armor that God provides: truth, righteousness, peace, faith, salvation, and the Word of God.

JESUS' CALL TO "FOLLOW"

Then he said to them all: "Whoever wants to be my disciple must deny themselves and take up their cross daily and follow me."

LUKE 9:23 NIV

The word *disciple* is defined as someone who learns from another person. Being a disciple of Jesus means receiving His teaching and learning from Him what it takes to please God.

Being Jesus' disciple doesn't mean you'll have an easy life. It may require facing struggles here on earth, and it might involve giving up some things you enjoy. That is why Jesus placed these conditions on true discipleship: "deny yourself," "take up your cross every day," and "follow Me."

Jesus is your Savior, your Lord, and your Friend. But He is also your Teacher and Leader, fully worthy of your studious attention every single day.

JESUS, OUR FOCUS

Wherefore seeing we also are compassed about with so great a cloud of witnesses, let us lay aside every weight, and the sin which doth so easily beset us, and let us run with patience the race that is set before us, looking unto Jesus the author and finisher of our faith; who for the joy that was set before him endured the cross, despising the shame, and is set down at the right hand of the throne of God. For consider him that endured such contradiction of sinners against himself, lest ye be wearied and faint in your minds.

HEBREWS 12:1–3 KJV

In this life, the temptations are great. As today's scripture makes clear, the temptations are great to justify our favorite sins and let our faith slide.

Therefore, keep "looking unto Jesus." Keep your eyes on the One whose love is the same yesterday, today, and forever (Hebrews 13:8). *Yesterday*, He paid for our salvation with His blood on the cross. *Today*, He intercedes for us before the Father. And *forever* He is ready to welcome and reward us in heaven.

CLASSICS: CHARLES H. SPURGEON

GOD DEFENDS HIS OWN

Asshur shall not save us; we will not ride upon horses:
neither will we say any more to the work of our hands,
Ye are our gods: for in thee the fatherless findeth mercy.

HOSEA 14:3 KJV

The Lord God of Israel, the one only living and true God, has this for a special mark of His character, that in Him the fatherless findeth mercy. "A Father of the fatherless, and a Judge of the widows, is God in his holy habitation." False gods of the heathen are usually notable for their supposed power or cunning, or even for their wickedness, falsehood, lustfulness and cruelty; but our God, who made the heavens, is the Thrice Holy One. He is the holy God, and He is also full of love.

Indeed, it is not only His name and His character, but His very nature, for "God is love." Among the acts which exhibit His love is this—that He executeth righteousness and judgment for all that are oppressed, and specially takes under His wing the defenseless ones, such as the widow and the fatherless.

A GOD WE CAN SEEK

*And that prophet, or that dreamer of dreams, shall be put
to death; because he hath spoken to turn you away from the
Lord your God, which brought you out of the land of Egypt, and
redeemed you out of the house of bondage, to thrust thee out
of the way which the Lord thy God commanded thee to walk
in. So shalt thou put the evil away from the midst of thee.*

DEUTERONOMY 13:5 KJV

We do not need false prophets to guide us away from God. We were born with a sin nature, bent towards self-satisfaction, the quest for which will always result in frustration and death. We were not made to be satisfied by anything less than God's presence.

When God changes our nature through Jesus' sacrifice, enabling our pursuit of Him, we must not turn away. God is opposed to those who would turn His people against Him. This is why the punishment for false prophets in Old Testament times was death.

Seek God. Don't turn aside toward the death trap of self-satisfaction. Just seek God.

GOD LOVES HUMILITY

Seek the LORD, all who are humble, and follow his commands. Seek to do what is right and to live humbly.

ZEPHANIAH 2:3 NLT

Humility can be an elusive target. The simple act of taking aim is a pretty good indication you're doing something wrong. And if you do hit the mark, as soon as you tell someone, you've turned that bull's-eye into an epic miss.

How is personal humility relevant in a world that places such high value on unending applause? Jesus' triumphal entry into Jerusalem provides us with a perfect example.

Imagine you've been cast to play a part in that scene. The lights come up. The city is electric. The crowd cheers wildly. When you play your part correctly, you eventually realize the applause you heard was not for you. In fact, most people won't even remember you were there.

Why? Because when you seek to do what is right and live humbly before God, you are not the coming King. You are the donkey.

GOD DEMANDS FORGIVERS

"Forgive us our sins, as we forgive those who sin against us."

LUKE 11:4 NLV

We take breaking God's laws pretty seriously, especially when someone else's lawbreaking impacts *us*. When wrong is done to you, it hurts. However, we might take sin a bit more lightly when we're the ones breaking a law of God. After all, He forgives us when we confess our sin, when we admit that He is right and we were wrong. We could even come to believe that our sin is no big deal to God. But that is far from the truth.

If you find yourself offended when someone breaks one of God's laws, you have only a small picture of how much sin offends God. He can and will, however, forgive. Will you? That's the point of the scripture above. If God's forgiveness is important to you, then follow His example—forgive others who've offended you.

CLASSICS: ANDREW MURRAY

GOD LONGS AND DELIGHTS TO BLESS YOU

The LORD thy God in the midst of thee is mighty; he will save, he will rejoice over thee with joy; he will rest in his love, he will joy over thee with singing.

ZEPHANIAH 3:17 KJV

Look up and see the great God upon His throne. He is Love—an unceasing and inexpressible desire to communicate His own goodness and blessedness to all His creatures. He longs and delights to bless. He has inconceivably glorious purposes concerning every one of His children, by the power of His Holy Spirit, to reveal in them His love and power. He waits with all the longings of a father's heart. He waits that He may be gracious unto you.

And each time you come to wait upon Him or seek to maintain in daily life the holy habit of waiting, you may look up and see Him ready to meet you, waiting that He may be gracious unto you. Yes, connect every exercise, every breath of the life of waiting, with faith's vision of your God waiting for you.

GOD'S HOLINESS

*God's discipline is always good for us,
so that we might share in his holiness.*

HEBREWS 12:10 NLT

The word *holy* and its synonyms appear more than sixteen hundred times throughout the Bible. It quickly becomes clear that God is holy, people aren't; God expects us to be holy, but we can't without His divine transformation.

After giving the Ten Commandments, the Lord told His ancient people: "Do not profane my holy name, for I must be acknowledged as holy by the Israelites. I am the LORD, who made you holy" (Leviticus 22:32 NIV). He also told them: "Be holy because I, the LORD your God, am holy" (Leviticus 19:2 NIV). Old and New Testament heroes of faith talk about the dichotomies of holiness, which both challenged them and spurred their faith into action.

Does God's glory and purity permeate your life? Yes! Now is the time to confess any known sin and embrace God's holiness anew.

GOD'S GENEROSITY

"In any of the towns in your land the Lord your God is giving you, if there is anyone poor among you, do not let your heart be hard and not be willing to help him. Be free to give to him. Let him use what is yours of anything he needs."

DEUTERONOMY 15:7–8 NLV

Generosity pays forward. It gives without expectation of repayment, and it starts with the realization that God has been generous toward us.

Consider today's scripture. The promised land was a fruitful place God gave to the Israelites not because they deserved His good gifts—remember, they were a stubborn people—but because God is generous. From that gift, God tells His people to give freely to the poor, to let them use whatever they need.

Whatever God has blessed you with, be generous toward others. Help when you can. Give without expecting anything in return. Remember the generosity that you've already received, and pay it forward.

WHAT'S MOST IMPORTANT

"Beware! Guard against every kind of greed.
Life is not measured by how much you own."

LUKE 12:15 NLT

When you encounter a Beware! sign, it's usually because there's danger ahead. This type of warning should cause you to stop and think about what you're about to do.

Jesus provides such a sign, connecting the warning to greed. Every possible species of greed carries danger with it. If you think you could finally be happy if you only had a particular thing, Jesus disagrees: "Life is not measured by how much you own."

It's very telling that the God who owns everything believes there's more to life than those earthly "things." The God who made Niagara Falls and Mount Everest thinks you're more important—and He wants to be most important to you also.

CLASSICS: D. L. MOODY

IF WE WILL ONLY BE LED BY JESUS

Likewise when the LORD sent you from Kadeshbarnea, saying, Go up and possess the land which I have given you; then ye rebelled against the commandment of the LORD your God, and ye believed him not, nor hearkened to his voice.

DEUTERONOMY 9:23 KJV

Who could lead the children of Israel through the wilderness like the Almighty God Himself?. . .It is true that if it had not been for their accursed unbelief they might have crossed into the land at Kadesh Barnea and taken possession of it, but they desired something besides God's word; so they were turned back and had to wander in the desert for forty years.

I believe there are thousands of God's children wandering in the wilderness still. The Lord has delivered them from the hand of the Egyptian and would at once take them through the wilderness right into the Promised Land if they were only willing to follow Christ. Christ has been down here and has made the rough places smooth, and the dark places light, and the crooked places straight. If we will only be led by Him and will follow Him, all will be peace and joy and rest.

WHEN GOD ALLOWS YOU TO BE TESTED

The testing of your faith produces perseverance.
Let perseverance finish its work so that you may
be mature and complete, not lacking anything.

JAMES 1:3–4 NIV

Ever wish life were easier? Actually, a too-easy life in a broken world probably would deaden our souls. James certainly knew that life is filled with temptations, trials, and tests of many kinds. While he wasn't one of the twelve apostles, James was a half-brother of Jesus who came to faith immediately after the Lord's resurrection.

Not surprisingly, many verses in James echo important themes Jesus discussed in the four Gospels. If you read the words of Jesus and the letter of James side by side, you can find more than three dozen common ideas.

Among them: learn to persevere in order to become Christlike. Or, as today's scripture says in the New Life Version, "Learn well how to wait [patiently endure] so you will be strong and complete and in need of nothing."

GOD IS BIGGER THAN OUR FEARS

"So be strong and courageous! Do not be afraid and do not panic before them. For the Lord your God will personally go ahead of you. He will neither fail you nor abandon you."

DEUTERONOMY 31:6 NLT

Fear can make giants out of anything. Courage will make those giants beatable. Wisdom is knowing that no giant is larger than the God who goes before you.

If the promised land had not been filled with strong, capable people who knew how to work the land and defend the goodness of the earth, it wouldn't have been worth God's promise. But when the Israelites saw the land's inhabitants, they quailed in the face of their opposition. They forgot that God was larger than their enemies, that He was larger than their fears.

Promised lands do not come without opposition, but God will never abandon you. Be strong and courageous! For the Lord your God goes with you.

GOD LOVES CHILDREN—
AND THE CHILDLIKE

Jesus called the children to him and said, "Let the little children come to me, and do not hinder them, for the kingdom of God belongs to such as these."

LUKE 18:16 NIV

In today's scripture, Jesus teaches two important lessons, the most obvious being that we should never hinder children from coming to Him—or even fail to show them the way. Children were never a bother to the Son of God!

The second lesson—and it's an important one to men of all ages—is contained in Jesus' words, "the kingdom of God belongs to such as these."

Such as these. The three words imply that, in order to inherit God's kingdom, we need to come to Jesus with faith like that of a little child. In other words, God honors the kind of faith that innocently and without self-justification comes to Him, empty hands outstretched. True faith is knowing we have nothing to offer to God but everything to receive in return.

CLASSICS: CHARLES H. SPURGEON

GOD NEVER SPENDS HIS STRENGTH

He that sitteth in the heavens shall laugh:
the Lord shall have them in derision.

PSALM 2:4 KJV

The great God can do all things without help. He needs no assistance from any created thing; indeed, there could be no such aid, since all the power of all other beings is derived from Himself alone. Creatures do not contribute to His strength; they only manifest Him . . . . To achieve any purpose of His heart He asketh none to be His ally, for alone He doeth as He wills.

What is more, He could with equal ease accomplish all His purposes if all created intelligences and forces were against Him. It would make no difference to His supremacy of might though all the tremendous powers which have now been created should revolt; He that sitteth in the heavens would have them in derision. Even powers which set up their standard against Him are beneath His control: His enemies are His footstool, out of their rage He bringeth forth His peaceful purposes. . . . Note well that when God hath done all that He pleaseth He hath not spent His strength.

INVISIBLE, YET SEEABLE

By faith he left Egypt, not fearing the king's anger;
he persevered because he saw him who is invisible.

HEBREWS 11:27 NIV

As physical beings in a tangible world, we human beings like things we can touch and see. The idea of an invisible, otherworldly God poses challenges to the human mind—why else would the Bible emphasize faith so heavily?

But we accept all kinds of invisible realities. The wind, sound waves, gravity, time—we can't see any of them, but we know they're real. And how about love, anger, jealousy, or joy? They are invisible forces often more powerful than physical ones.

God is the most powerful invisible force of all. But though we can't see Him, we can certainly see His effects in the world. Today's scripture describes Moses' perception of the invisible God, which encouraged him to accomplish great things by faith.

We can too. God is seeable in His creation, His Word, and His movement in the lives of people and nations. Just look for Him, and see what He'll do in your life.

A GOD-ORDAINED PATH

"Do two walk together unless they have agreed to do so?"

AMOS 3:3 NIV

It has been said that a journey of a thousand miles begins with a single step. And while no journey of any kind can begin without the courage to move forward, the important question remains: Where are we going?

God has a path for each of us to follow, a path that requires that we follow Him daily. So are we walking along the path He has for us today? Or are we leaning on something or someone else for wisdom and direction? If so, it's time to put down that crutch and discover what God can do.

Jesus said, "I am the light of the world. Whoever follows me will never walk in darkness, but will have the light of life" (John 8:12 NIV). Walking with Jesus is the single most important course we can take in this life. That road, and the destination it leads to, are absolutely worth the effort.

THE SOVEREIGN MASTER

For, lo, I raise up the Chaldeans, that bitter and hasty nation, which shall march through the breadth of the land, to possess the dwellingplaces that are not their's.

HABAKKUK 1:6 KJV

The Babylonians—sometimes called the Chaldeans— were a fearsome nation that would eventually storm Judah and take it by force. However, even while the Babylonians were plotting their strategies, God was pulling the strings. Their empire eventually fell to the Persians, who then fell to the Greeks, who were later replaced by the Romans, under whose reign Jesus—the King of kings—was born.

As Daniel said, God "changeth the times and the seasons: he removeth kings, and setteth up kings" (2:21 KJV). When chaos seems to reign, whether in the political climate or within our lives, God remains sovereign. Nothing takes Him by surprise because He's the One directing it all—even the actions of our enemies.

God works behind the scenes, subtly but consistently tugging the line of history toward eternity.

CLASSICS: CHARLES H. SPURGEON

GOD DOES WHAT IS GOOD IN HIS SIGHT

*Is it not lawful for me to do what I will with
mine own? Is thine eye evil, because I am good?*

MATTHEW 20:15 KJV

I shall dwell only upon one portion of God's sovereignty, and that is God's sovereignty in the distribution of His gifts. In this respect I believe He has a right to do as He wills with His own and that He exercises that right. We must assume. . .that all blessings are gifts and that we have no claim to them by our own merit. This, I think, every considerate mind will grant. And this being admitted, we shall endeavor to show that He has a right, seeing they are His own to do what He wills with them—to withhold them wholly as He pleaseth—to distribute them all if He chooseth—to give to some and not to others—to give to none or to give to all, just as seemeth good in His sight. "Is it not lawful for me to do what I will with mine own?"

NO SPACE BETWEEN FATHER AND SON

The Word (Christ) was in the beginning. The Word was with God. The Word was God. He was with God in the beginning.

JOHN 1:1–2 NLV

It was important to God that the connection between Father and Son be established in scripture. He wanted people to know that the Father and Jesus are one—that they have both always existed, that Jesus was there when the world was made.

That's an impressive resume, but why is it important that we know that? Because it shows that anything Jesus said was from the mouth of God Himself. Yes, Jesus came in the form of man, but He did not give up the authority He always had. Jesus didn't always use His authority here on earth, but it was His all the same.

When you read the teaching and instruction of Jesus, you are reading the teaching and instruction of God. There is no space between Father and Son.

WHEN GOD'S COMMANDS DON'T MAKE SENSE

So the people called out and the religious leaders blew the horns. When the people heard the sound of the horns, they called out even louder. And the wall fell to the ground. All the people went straight in and took the city.

JOSHUA 6:20 NLV

Sometimes, God's instructions don't make sense. For six days, Joshua led the Israelite men of war around the fortified city of Jericho. On the seventh day, they circled the city seven times, culminating in the walls of Jericho falling as horns blew and people shouted.

God didn't need a full week to hand Joshua victory over Jericho. He could have crushed the city on day one. God invited Joshua to trust Him, to follow His instructions—even if they seemed strange—in order to show that He keeps His promises.

When God's instructions don't make sense, when you are told to turn the other cheek, to be generous, or to tithe your paycheck toward ministry, trust God. Allow your self-made defenses to fall so you can see God's deliverance.

A HEAVEN-SENT TEACHER

After dark one evening, [Nicodemus] came to speak with Jesus.
"Rabbi," he said, "we all know that God has sent you to teach
us. Your miraculous signs are evidence that God is with you."

JOHN 3:2 NLT

A skeptic looked at the evidence and concluded God was with Jesus. So he came to ask the one he recognized as a heaven-sent teacher. Nicodemus, a man who only knew religious law, sought out Jesus and brought questions in need of answers. Nicodemus was a teacher, leader, and ruler who knew the law, but Jesus introduced concepts that were foreign to him.

Nicodemus would learn. He found reason to believe. He began to see that there was a difference between following the rules and honoring the Rule Maker.

You have the same opportunity. You can live with what you think you know about God, or you can recognize Jesus as God's gift to you and learn from Him. You may find that there is a difference between what you understand and His definitive truth.

CLASSICS: D. L. MOODY

OBEY GOD IN THE DARK

And [God] said, Take now thy son, thine only son Isaac, whom thou lovest, and get thee into the land of Moriah; and offer him there for a burnt offering upon one of the mountains which I will tell thee of. And Abraham rose up early in the morning, and saddled his ass, and took two of his young men with him, and Isaac his son, and clave the wood for the burnt offering, and rose up, and went unto the place of which God had told him.

GENESIS 22:2–3 KJV

Would that there were more men now like Abraham, ready to obey God in the dark without asking the reason why. The old man took his son, and he told him the secret that he had hid from him all the journey— that God had told him to offer him up as a sacrifice; and he bound the boy hand and foot and laid him all ready on the altar. But just as he was about to stretch forth his hand and slay him, he heard a voice from heaven calling to him, "Abraham, Abraham, spare thy son." God was more merciful to the son of Abraham than to His own Son, for He gave Him up freely for us all.

JESUS SATISFIES THE SOUL

Jesus answered her, "If you knew the gift of God and who it is that asks you for a drink, you would have asked him and he would have given you living water."

JOHN 4:10 NIV

Jesus met all kinds of people. If you read enough of His interactions with them, you might see yourself in some of those personalities. In the verse above, Jesus is speaking to a Samaritan woman. She was an outcast, viewed as disreputable. She had a need for healing—she was weary and her soul was dry. She was curious.

When Jesus asked this woman for a drink, it was so He could introduce her to the possibility of lasting satisfaction—*soul* satisfaction. He offered something she had never known—a consistent refreshing of the soul. This was living water that could saturate, bringing a life purpose so many miss.

Do you know this kind of refreshment? Have you asked for it? Will you?

SUFFERING LIKE JESUS

These things are all a part of the Christian life to which you have been called. Christ suffered for us. This shows us we are to follow in His steps.

1 PETER 2:21 NLV

The apostle Peter intertwines three important themes throughout his first letter. With the first, he emphasizes how much we have received and have to look forward to for all eternity thanks to the Gospel of Jesus Christ. In the second, he emphasizes how Jesus Christ set the standard for us if we're called to suffer on earth. In the third, Peter emphasizes our need to live under authority, both good and bad.

In today's scripture, Peter calls for an immediate response. Will you say yes, telling the Lord, "I choose to follow Jesus Christ's example and am willing to suffer for doing right"? If so, you're on the path to true Christlikeness.

EQUAL-OPPORTUNITY GOD

Now Deborah, a prophet, the wife of Lappidoth, was leading Israel at that time. She held court under the Palm of Deborah between Ramah and Bethel in the hill country of Ephraim, and the Israelites went up to her to have their disputes decided.

JUDGES 4:4–5 NIV

God is an equal-opportunity deliverer. He gives wisdom to all who ask, and He enables women and men alike to lead according to His design.

Deborah, the only female judge of Israel, was known for wise judgment as she led Israel to victory over its oppressors by faithfully communicating God's instructions to His people.

By contrast, Samson, the strongman judge, repeatedly violated his Nazarite vow and flirted with the enemy, literally bringing disaster upon himself as well as his enemies.

God will achieve His goals, and He'll use the people He wants to use. But it will always go better for those who follow Him willingly and are faithful to His instructions.

CLASSICS: CHARLES H. SPURGEON

BE WATCHING FOR JESUS' RETURN

When the Son of man shall come in his glory, and all the holy angels with him, then shall he sit upon the throne of his glory.

MATTHEW 25:31 KJV

We are told that [Jesus] will come quickly. It seems a long time since that was said, even eighteen hundred years, but we remember that things which are slow with us may be very quick with the Lord; for one day with the Lord is as a thousand years, and a thousand years as one day. It is not for us to know the times and the seasons; they remain hidden in the purpose of God.

For excellent reasons these times and seasons are unrevealed, that we may be always on the watchtower, not knowing at what hour the Lord Jesus may be revealed. To the ungodly world He will come as a thief in the night and take them at unawares; but we, brethren, are not in darkness that that day should overtake us as a thief. Being children of the day, we are taught to be wakeful, and, standing in the clear light with our loins girt, we ought to be always looking for our Master's appearing.

THE GIVER OF LASTING LIFE

"For sure, I tell you, anyone who hears My Word and puts his trust in Him Who sent Me has life that lasts forever. . . . He has already passed from death into life."

JOHN 5:24 NLV

Is life only the distance between first and last breath? Is death the end of that cycle? In a purely physical sense, the answer is yes. But there is more to real life than physical breath. Please consider one more question: "What comes next?"

Jesus gave a simple and concise overview of the truth about life. When you hear what He said, when you trust in the God who sent Him, you are given the gift of life beyond your last breath. In fact, this everlasting and forever life begins the moment you do. This is God's gift to you. Share this truth—this good news—with others so they can make the choice to follow the One who delivers real and lasting life.

GOD REQUIRES HONESTY AND FAIRNESS

Hear this, you who trample the needy and do away with the poor of the land, saying, "When will the New Moon be over that we may sell grain, and the Sabbath be ended that we may market wheat?"— skimping on the measure, boosting the price and cheating with dishonest scales, buying the poor with silver and the needy for a pair of sandals, selling even the sweepings with the wheat."

AMOS 8:4–6 NIV

The prophet Amos wasn't afraid to offend anyone, including the rich and influential. In today's scripture, he spoke out very harshly against those who made their money by treating the poor and vulnerable unfairly.

God is and always has been concerned with the plight of the poor and disadvantaged, which is partly why He gave His people what Jesus called one of the two most important commandments: "Love your neighbor as yourself" (Matthew 22:39).

Do you want to show your love for God? Make sure you always treat people justly and honestly.

GOD'S STRENGTH

Each of you should use whatever gift you have received to serve others, as faithful stewards of God's grace in its various forms. If anyone speaks, they should do so as one who speaks the very words of God. If anyone serves, they should do so with the strength God provides, so that in all things God may be praised through Jesus Christ. To him be the glory and the power for ever and ever. Amen.

1 PETER 4:10–11 NIV

The Lord God wants us to frequently ask for His strength to live our lives on this earth. The scripture above includes not just praise to God (the ending doxology), but a seeking of Him, a rejoicing in Him, and gratitude to Him—in advance—for what He's going to do.

These activities tend to go together, don't they? It's what many Bible teachers of past generations called "the normal Christian life." Why not make it yours?

CLASSICS: CHARLES H. SPURGEON

LOOK BACK TO UNDERSTAND JESUS

*Speak unto the children of Israel, that they bring thee
a red heifer without spot, wherein is no blemish, and
upon which never came yoke: and ye shall give her unto
Eleazar the priest, that he may bring her forth without
the camp, and one shall slay her before his face.*

NUMBERS 19:2–3 KJV

To the Israelites, these rites must have been rather an exercise of faith. . . . "I cannot perfectly understand why this heifer is slain, or why yonder lamb is offered," said the pious Israelite, "but. . .I reverently do, even to the smallest particular, that which God, through His servant Moses, has commanded me to do." . . . Having believed in Christ Jesus, having received Him as the Father's sent One and being reconciled unto God by His death, we look back to the ceremonies of the old law as the patterns of heavenly things, to endeavor to discover some new light in which the Savior's beauties may be set and to behold Him from some different point of view, so that we may love Him better and trust Him more.

GOD KNOWS OUR MOTIVES

They answered, "Show us a miraculous sign if you want us to believe in you. What can you do?"

JOHN 6:30 NLT

The scripture above does not show honor. It's a challenge. It's a threat. It's defiance. The people gathered to see Jesus perform on demand. He had the crowd, but they wanted Him to impress them by raising the bar. If Jesus would feed them, heal them, and eliminate their enemies. . .then they might follow Him.

Jesus recognized the needs, but He also recognized the motives. The people were only willing to come out and see Him each day if He provided them food and health. They wanted those two things more than they wanted what He could teach them—more than they wanted *Him*. If the Son of God wouldn't do what they asked, then He wasn't worth following.

Don't fall into this trap. God does not exist to remove all struggle but to help you *through* the struggle. He may not remove pain, but He will give you the tools to deal with the pain. He offers so much more than physical blessings.

A WELCOMING SAVIOR

*For if you do these things, you will never stumble,
and you will receive a rich welcome into the eternal
kingdom of our Lord and Savior Jesus Christ.*

2 PETER 1:10–11 NIV

The apostle Peter never stopped growing in his faith, commitment, and overflowing love for Jesus Christ. In the end, he willingly died as a martyr. And Peter could do those things because he had an assurance of his place in God's eternal kingdom.

No doubt the apostle remembered this precious promise from Jesus, who had come to earth to make a way for his salvation—and the salvation of all who would believe in Him: "My Father's house has many rooms; if that were not so, would I have told you that I am going there to prepare a place for you? And if I go and prepare a place for you, I will come back and take you to be with me that you also may be where I am" (John 14:2–3 NIV).

If you know and follow Jesus, you can be assured that He will richly welcome you into His Father's eternal kingdom.

GOD RUNS AHEAD OF YOUR PRAYER

*"Before they call I will answer;
while they are still speaking I will hear."*

ISAIAH 65:24 NIV

Today's scripture is part of an end-times prophecy that Isaiah delivered on God's behalf. A day would come, the Lord promised, when a new heaven and new earth would contain a restored Jerusalem, when He would delight in His people, when He would oversee peace and prosperity and answered prayer—even before the prayer was spoken!

For Christians today, Isaiah 65:24 provides a glimpse of our God's knowledge and power. If He can answer prayers before they're prayed in the future, He can also do that now. "I the Lord do not change," God said through the prophet Malachi (3:6 NIV)—so His powers then are His powers now are His powers in all times.

Knowing that, don't ever worry that you're on your own. God is there, listening for your prayer, even running ahead of your prayers to help you. Just be sure to pray.

CLASSICS: CHARLES H. SPURGEON

PRAYER, OUR CONSTANT COMPANION

And in the morning, rising up a great while before day, he went out, and departed into a solitary place, and there prayed.

MARK 1:35 KJV

I delight to think of our Lord as praying before He did a great thing: it was His custom so to do.

When the blessing has really come, and souls are being saved on all sides, then we are to redouble our cries to heaven, that the merciful presence may be retained and enjoyed to a still higher degree. Fresh from the wonderful successes of that miraculous night, the Christ of God goes on the Sunday morning to open the gates of the day with the uplifted hands of His prayer.

Prayer should be our companion at all times. Pray when you are pining for a blessing; pray when you have newly obtained a blessing.

THE GOD WHO JUDGES EVIL

"At that time I will deal with all who oppressed you. I will rescue the lame; I will gather the exiles. I will give them praise and honor in every land where they have suffered shame."

ZEPHANIAH 3:19 NIV

The world can sometimes feel like an inverted courtroom in which the wicked sit smugly in the jury while the righteous wither under their gaze. Evil gets a free pass while holiness is denied, and the sacred is trod under foot by the profane.

God hears each one of our pleas for justice, and He feels our pain because He too was despised. "You will be hated by everyone because of me," Jesus told His disciples (Matthew 10:22 NIV). Satan loathes the Gospel message because it proclaims his ultimate defeat—and he'll do anything to stop you from spreading it. The second half of Jesus' warning, however, offers us hope: "The one who stands firm to the end will be saved."

The courts won't be flipped for long—the true Judge is coming.

JESUS' FAMOUS LAST WORDS

Jesus said, "It is finished." With that,
he bowed his head and gave up his spirit.

JOHN 19:30 NIV

Spikes were driven through Jesus' flesh, securing Him to crude wooden beams—and this after devastating beatings and the placing of a crown made from thorn spikes onto the skin of His head. He would have been weak from blood loss, and in the end the human body of Jesus would draw the last breath of physical life.

Jesus came to do something only He could do, and His last words were a proclamation not of defeat but triumph: "It is finished."

God wanted to reclaim souls that found a home in human flesh. When the end came for every person, God wanted them to move home with Him. You were on God's mind when this reclaiming process—also known as redemption—was taking place on the cross. Without it, lost men would stay lost. With it, they can inherit a forever home with God.

GOD SEES WHAT YOU CAN BECOME

Then the angel of the LORD came and sat beneath the great tree at Ophrah, which belonged to Joash of the clan of Abiezer. Gideon son of Joash was threshing wheat at the bottom of a winepress to hide the grain from the Midianites. The angel of the LORD appeared to him and said, "Mighty hero, the LORD is with you!"

JUDGES 6:11–12 NLT

Imagine you're so afraid of the enemy that you thresh your grain at the bottom of a winepress. Now imagine an angel of the Lord appears and calls you a "mighty hero." You'd probably wonder if the angel had the right guy.

God sees beyond our current condition to the potential within. Our potential for becoming mighty heroes isn't determined by our own latent resolve. It comes from relying on God to be strong in our weakness.

Just as Gideon was able to lead Israel to miraculous military victory, you can have victory when you allow God to tap into the potential He's given you.

CLASSICS: ANDREW MURRAY

DO AS GOD SAYS

So Abram departed, as the LORD had spoken unto him.

GENESIS 12:4 KJV

How well the Old Testament saints understood this connection between God's words and ours, and how really prayer with them was the loving response to what they had heard God speak! If the word were a promise, they counted *on God to do as He had spoken.* "Do as Thou hast said"; "For Thou, Lord, hast spoken it"; "According to Thy promise"; "According to Thy word": in such expressions they showed that what God spake in promise was the root and the life of what they spake in prayer. If the word was a command, they simply *did as the Lord had spoken:* "So Abram departed as the Lord had spoken." Their life was fellowship with God, the interchange of word and thought. What God spoke they heard and did; what they spoke God heard and did. In each word He speaks to us, the whole Christ gives Himself to fulfill it for us. For each word He asks no less that we give the whole man to keep that word and to receive its fulfillment.

A PURPOSE-GIVING SAVIOR

Then Jesus said to them again, "May you have peace. As the Father has sent Me, I also am sending you."

JOHN 20:21 NLV

This is a pivot point based on the knowledge that Jesus had risen from the dead. He'd finished the work God had given Him to do. The disciples had gone from feelings of complete and utter loss to a full-on struggle with disbelief. People didn't just rise from the dead, but they had seen it—both when Jesus brought Lazarus back to life after four days in the grave and when He came back from the dead Himself. Jesus had that kind of power.

Now? He would send the disciples in the same way God the Father had sent Him. God sent Jesus and Jesus sent the disciples. He wouldn't leave them to walk alone. While they wouldn't have the benefit of His physical presence, they would have His peace, His plan, and His Spirit.

As Jesus sent His disciples, He also sends you—and with the same tools. Embrace these words from Jesus: "I am sending you." That's purpose!

GOD'S TOP PRIORITY

This is what the Lord Almighty says: "These people say, 'The time has not yet come to rebuild the Lord's house.'" Then the word of the Lord came through the prophet Haggai: "Is it a time for you yourselves to be living in your paneled houses, while this house remains a ruin?"

HAGGAI 1:2–4 NIV

The book of Haggai teaches us Christian men the importance of priorities—specifically *God's* priorities. It opens with the prophet chiding builders who had delayed in doing the work God had given them to do—rebuilding the temple in Jerusalem—to instead focus on constructing their own homes.

Life is filled with important tasks, and each of us needs to learn to set priorities. But we do well to remember that our God loves us deeply and wants us to place our relationship with Him above all other things—no matter how important they may seem.

God so wanted a mutually loving relationship with us that He sent His Son to earth to make it happen. Knowing that, we should make Him our very first priority.

GOD'S HEART FOR THE LOST

The Lord is not slow in keeping his promise, as some understand slowness. Instead he is patient with you, not wanting anyone to perish, but everyone to come to repentance.

2 PETER 3:9 NIV

The last words of the apostle Peter bear deep consideration. What is utmost on his mind at the end of his second epistle? First, that we keep taking God at His word, that we cling to it, that we believe what He has said, and that we not be carried away by false teaching. Second, that we live pure lives, keeping our eyes on eternity—not on what is temporal and soon to fade away.

Then third, in today's scripture, we see Peter echoing God's own heart. Throughout scripture, the foremost theme is God's desire to reconcile individuals to Himself. That's why the Bible says repeatedly that the Lord doesn't want anyone to perish but all to come to repentance. When you pray earnestly for someone's salvation, God says, "Amen."

CLASSICS: JOHN WESLEY

A TRUE BENEFIT OF FEAR

And I say unto you my friends, Be not afraid of them that kill the body, and after that have no more that they can do. But I will forewarn you whom ye shall fear: Fear him, which after he hath killed hath power to cast into hell; yea, I say unto you, Fear him.

LUKE 12:4–5 KJV

Every truth which is revealed in the oracles of God is undoubtedly of great importance. Yet it may be allowed that some of those which are revealed therein are of greater importance than others, as being more immediately conducive to the grand end of all, the eternal salvation of men. . . . And let it not be thought that the consideration of these terrible truths is proper only for enormous sinners. How is this supposition consistent with what our Lord speaks to those who were then, doubtless, the holiest men upon earth? . . .

Yea, fear Him under this very notion, of having power to cast into hell: That is, in effect, fear lest He should cast you into the place of torment. And this very fear, even in the children of God, is one excellent means of preserving them from it.

JESUS' RETURN

"Jesus has been taken from you into heaven, but someday he will return from heaven in the same way you saw him go!"

ACTS 1:11 NLT

God did not send Jesus into our world so He could know from experience what it was like to be human. God the Father had planned a rescue mission from all eternity, and only Jesus met the qualifications to lead the expedition. He came, He taught, He died, and He came back to life. Then Jesus returned to be with His Father.

But in the scripture above, we read of a future day—a day only God knows—when Jesus will come to earth again. He has been preparing for that day and while His family grows here on earth.

God has given you something to look forward to, a hope to cling to, and a promise to remember. He loves you enough to care for you now—and to prepare you for your perfect eternity.

You have not been stranded. Jesus is coming back!

A GOD WHO TRANSFORMS

Naomi took the baby and cuddled him to her breast. And she cared for him as if he were her own. The neighbor women said, "Now at last Naomi has a son again!" And they named him Obed. He became the father of Jesse and the grandfather of David.

RUTH 4:16–17 NLT

In the light of eternity, a time of grief is but a bitter blink of the eye. Consider Naomi, whose husband and sons died while in Moab. Her grief was so great that she wanted to change her name to Mara, which means "bitter" (see Ruth 1:20).

Naomi didn't understand why God would bring such misfortune upon her, but God had a plan. In order for Ruth—Naomi's Moabite daughter-in-law—to become the great-grandmother of King David, Naomi and Ruth needed to leave Moab and seek assistance from a kinsman named Boaz. The love story that followed led to Ruth's redemption and to the return of Naomi's joy.

In times of grief, don't lose hope. God can transform your bitterness into redemptive joy.

GOD WANTS FELLOWSHIP WITH US

We proclaim to you what we have seen and heard, so that you also may have fellowship with us. And our fellowship is with the Father and with his Son, Jesus Christ.

1 JOHN 1:3 NIV

In the New Testament, the word *fellowship* refers to a sharing bond of love between two persons. Fellow Christians are encouraged to spend time with one, enjoying "fellowship" with one another in Christ. Then they can challenge and encourage each other in their walk of faith.

In today's scripture, the apostle John refers to Christians' fellowship not just with one another but with God the Father and with Jesus Christ, His Son.

God is our Creator, but He wants so much more. He invites us to enjoy a loving, sharing, intimate bond with Himself. How will you respond to that invitation today—and every day?

CLASSICS: CHARLES H. SPURGEON

BRING THE KING BACK

And Absalom, whom we anointed over us, is dead in battle. Now therefore why speak ye not a word of bringing the king back?

2 SAMUEL 19:10 KJV

Many among us have lost the comfortable presence of the Lord Jesus Christ. Some have long dwelt in the cold shade of suspended fellowship; others for a shorter period have passed through the cloud; but, surely, the shortest period is all too long—and those who have lost fellowship must be anxiously pining after its restoration. Now to such as these, who see no longer the bright and morning star, we say, "Why speak ye not a word of bringing the King back?"

My sorrowing brother, you have been mourning much concerning your present condition; sitting down, perhaps, this very afternoon and taking stock of your spiritual estate, you have felt yourself to be in an almost bankrupt condition, and you have written bitter things against yourself. . . . You observe that your prayers have not been so constant nor so fervent as they used to be. In reading the Word, the promises have not been laid home to your heart as once they were, and . . . All because your eyes have not lately seen the King in His beauty.

BECAUSE HE LOVES, GOD IS GENEROUS

Joseph, a Levite from Cyprus, whom the apostles called Barnabas (which means "son of encouragement"), sold a field he owned and brought the money and put it at the apostles' feet.

ACTS 4:36–37 NIV

Barnabas was a man who was useful to the apostle Paul on missions trips, but his first introduction was in today's scripture, which shows that he allowed godly generosity to rule his actions. Barnabas sold land he owned and then gave the entire purchase price to the apostles for the work they were doing.

God inspires that kind of generosity—and He demonstrates it too. Paul wrote that God "richly provides us with everything for our enjoyment" (1 Timothy 6:17 NIV) and that He will "meet all your needs according to the riches of his glory in Christ Jesus" (Philippians 4:19 NIV).

God is generous because He loves, and love always motivates generosity. And God's generosity toward us should motivate us to demonstrate that kind of generosity toward others.

GOD IS FAITHFUL TO FORGIVE

If we confess our sins, he [God] is faithful and just to forgive us our sins, and to cleanse us from all unrighteousness.

1 JOHN 1:9 KJV

The Christian faith is simple: "If thou shalt confess with thy mouth the Lord Jesus, and shalt believe in thine heart that God hath raised him from the dead, thou shalt be saved" (Romans 10:9 KJV). The Christian *life*, on the other hand, can be more complicated. Even after salvation, our "flesh" wars against our new spirit (1 Peter 2:11)—and one of the biggest battlegrounds is the area of forgiveness.

From our human perspective, it's tough to forgive offenses, whether truly life-altering sins committed against us or simply the day-to-day irritations that occur. But we must forgive because our God forgives— and our offenses against His holiness are massive and never-ending.

Here, we return to the simplicity of our faith. If we just confess our sins to God, if we agree with Him that we have done wrong, He will quickly and completely forgive us of them. This is a promise we are blessed to claim day after day, year after year.

A GIFT-GIVING GOD

"I prayed for this boy, and the Lord has given me what I asked of Him. So I have given him to the Lord. He is given to the Lord as long as he lives." And they worshiped the Lord there.

1 SAMUEL 1:27–28 NLV

God delights in giving good gifts to His children not so they will take joy in the gift but so they will worship the Giver.

Too often, our prayers resemble grocery lists of things we want, things we think will make us happy. And when God grants our requests, we rejoice in the wrong thing or think that thing is rightfully ours when it really still belongs to God.

Let Hannah be an example of how you should pray and worshipfully give back the gifts that God has given you. When God places a desire in your heart, pray about it. Ask Him to grant that desire. And when He gives you the desire of your heart, give it back to Him.

CLASSICS: ANDREW MURRAY

TAKE THE WORD INTO YOUR HEART

For I say unto you, that this that is written must yet be accomplished in me, And he was reckoned among the transgressors: for the things concerning me have an end.

LUKE 22:37 KJV

Do believe, every time you open your Bible, that just as sure as you listen to the divine, Spirit-breathed Word, so surely will our Father, in answer to the prayer of faith and docile waiting, give the Holy Spirit's living operation in your heart. Let all your Bible study be a thing of faith. Do not only try and believe the truths or promises you read. This may be in your own power. Before that, believe in the Holy Spirit, in His being in you, in God's working in you through Him. Take the Word into your heart, in the quiet faith that He will enable you to love it and yield to it and keep it; and our blessed Lord Jesus will make the book to you what it was to Him when He spoke of "the things which are written concerning Me." All scripture will become the simple revelation of what God is going to do for you, and in you, and through you.

GOD'S REST

There remains, then, a Sabbath-rest for the people of God; for anyone who enters God's rest also rests from their works, just as God did from his.

HEBREWS 4:9–10 NIV

Ever get tired? Of course. Physically, emotionally, spiritually. . .life can be exhausting.

When we were kids, we didn't notice the weariness so much. We played with seemingly limitless energy—until we crashed into bed at night. Young men often find that first full-time job surprisingly tiring. Building a career or business, serving in church, or raising kids of your own can sap your energies. The process of aging, which sneaks up on everyone, leaves us longing for a rest that refreshes.

God knows all these things, and He promises His children a perfect, perpetual rest. Though He never tires, He set the example of resting from work (Genesis 2:2–3). . .and He is planning a day when you too will enjoy a refreshment that never ends.

GOD IS OUR SOURCE

I will fill this house with glory, saith the LORD of hosts. The silver is mine, and the gold is mine. . . . The glory of this latter house shall be greater than of the former, saith the LORD of hosts: and in this place will I give peace.

HAGGAI 2:7–9 KJV

Centuries before Haggai's time, David wrote, "The earth is the LORD's, and everything in it, the world, and all who live in it; for he founded it on the seas and established it on the waters" (Psalm 24:1–2 NIV).

There is comfort in knowing that God is the owner of everything in this world, including the natural resources we use for creating useful things. We have the assurance that God Himself is our Source for all we need to accomplish the tasks He has set before us.

That is the message of hope and assurance the Lord gave His people as they set about rebuilding His temple. In effect, He told them, "I own all the resources; I am your Source." It's a message we should boldly receive for ourselves today.

THE ULTIMATE RULER

*The Lord will be King over all the earth. On that day the
Lord will be the only one, and His name the only one.*

ZECHARIAH 14:9 NLV

In medieval times, an errand from the king was treated
with utmost importance. Faithful servants either completed the task. . .or died trying.

The modern Church seems to have lessened its
view of God. How often do we treat His rules like mere
suggestions, only following them at convenient times?
Even worse, how often do we disregard His commands
out of fear that others will notice?

Throughout His Word, God refers to those who
speak against Him as "fools," so why should we fear
their opinions? The ground we walk upon belongs to
God, so it's time to start focusing on how to please the
King, not the court jesters.

Only when we place God at the top of our mental
hierarchy will our obedience flow naturally from our
heart's desire.

CLASSICS: D. L. MOODY

GOD HEARS YOUR PRAYERS

If my people, which are called by my name, shall humble themselves, and pray, and seek my face, and turn from their wicked ways; then will I hear from heaven, and will forgive their sin, and will heal their land.

2 CHRONICLES 7:14 KJV

God has a home, and heaven is His dwelling place. How far away that home of God, that heaven, is I do not know. But one thing I do know; it is not so far away but God can hear us when we pray. God can hear every prayer that goes up to Him there from this sin-cursed earth. We are not so far from Him but that He can see our tears and hear the faintest whisper when we lift our hearts to Him in prayer. Do we not read, "If My people, which are called by My name, shall humble themselves, and pray, and seek My face, and turn from their wicked ways, then will I hear from heaven, and will forgive their sin, and will heal their land." That is God's own word: "I will hear from heaven," and "I will forgive their sin."

THE POWER OF THE MESSAGE

"Leave these men alone. Let them go. If they are planning and doing these things merely on their own, it will soon be overthrown. But if it is from God, you will not be able to overthrow them. You may even find yourselves fighting against God!"

ACTS 5:38–39 NLT

The Jewish religious leaders were frustrated. They believed that Jesus' death would cause His followers to forget His teachings. But when that didn't happen, some of these leaders proposed harsh action.

One Pharisee, though, suggested that they just let Peter and the rest of the apostles speak their message. If it was from God, Gamaliel said, they wouldn't be able to stop it—nor should they try.

Peter's message, it turns out, *was* from God, and it was so powerful that nothing—religious opposition, Roman law, or persecution—could stop it.

The good news of salvation through faith in Jesus was a powerful, unstoppable message in Peter's day, and it still is today. It's God's message, which cannot be stopped.

A GOD WHO "CALLS" US

Then the Lord came and stood and called as He did the other times, "Samuel! Samuel!" And Samuel said, "Speak, for Your servant is listening."

1 SAMUEL 3:10 NLV

Samuel was the answer to the prayer of his mother, Hannah, and the gift she returned to God. He was raised in the temple by Eli, the priest.

Eli's sons, though also raised in the temple, were described as worthless men who didn't know the Lord (see 1 Samuel 2:12). So when Eli was old, God called Samuel to be His servant.

Samuel was already God's, given back to Him by Hannah, but God wanted Samuel to answer the call for Himself. Would Samuel have been called if he followed the path of Eli's worthless sons? Probably not.

To hear God's call, you must listen with a pure heart, dedicated to God alone. Can you hear Him? He's still calling.

GOD GIVES—HE NEVER SELLS

"Let me have this power, too," [Simon] exclaimed, "so that when I lay my hands on people, they will receive the Holy Spirit!"

ACTS 8:19 NLT

Simon the magician didn't know it, but what he was listening to and watching wasn't for sale. So instead of receiving what the apostles were offering, he sought to "buy" the power of the Holy Spirit. Peter's pointed response? "May your money be destroyed with you for thinking God's gift can be bought!" (Acts 8:20 NLT).

No part of God can be purchased or earned in any way. He's not for sale, rent, or lease. You can have Him in full, but you must believe and receive Him and all He offers as a free gift. It's not a matter of your ability to pay for or earn God's favor; it's a matter of His grace being fully poured out on you.

God gives—He never sells.

CLASSICS: D. L. MOODY

ALL THE LIGHT YOU NEED

Then spake Jesus again unto them, saying, I am the light of the world: he that followeth me shall not walk in darkness, but shall have the light of life.

JOHN 8:12 KJV

Christ is not only our way. He is the Light upon the way. He says, "I am the Light of the world." He goes on to say, "He that followeth Me shall not walk in darkness, but shall have the light of life." It is impossible for any man or woman who is following Christ to walk in darkness.

If your soul is in the darkness, groping around in the fog and mist of earth, let me tell you it is because you have got away from the true light. There is nothing but light that will dispel darkness. So let those who are walking in spiritual darkness admit Christ into their hearts: He is the Light.

GOD LOVES THE UNLIKELY

He fell to the ground and heard a voice saying to him,
"Saul! Saul! Why are you persecuting me?"

ACTS 9:4 NLT

Saul did not like Jesus, and he *hated* Jesus' followers—so much so that he was part of the mob that killed the early church deacon Stephen. Saul had gained a terrible reputation as a violent persecutor of the church. Yet Jesus met him on the road to Damascus and completely changed his thinking, his heart, and his course in life.

Why do you think Jesus would reach out to a man who was His sworn enemy? The answer is that Jesus saw Saul (later known as Paul) through the lens of what He had for him to do: to take the message of salvation to the whole world.

Paul later wrote that we were all at one time alienated from God—we were all His enemies—but that God brought us into His family through the death of Jesus Christ (see Colossians 1:21–22). All of us were born opposing God. But He can still use us to accomplish His purposes. Then, one day, He'll welcome each of us into His eternal kingdom.

LOVE COMES FROM GOD

Dear friends, let us love one another, for love comes from God. Everyone who loves has been born of God and knows God. Whoever does not love does not know God, because God is love.

1 JOHN 4:7–8 NIV

All of God's characteristics stretch across the hundred billion light-years of this universe. This is especially true of His love.

The terms *God* and *love* appear adjacent to each other many, many times throughout the Bible, especially in the New Testament. The most famous of those verses is John 3:16. Others include today's scripture, 1 John 4:9–12, 1 John 4:16, and 1 John 4:19–20.

It's great to know *about* God's love, but it's not enough. We must allow that love to become part of who we are in Christ. Does God's graciousness and passion permeate your life? It's there for the taking. Open your heart to receive His love right now.

GOD IS KING

"All right, here is the king you have chosen. You asked for him, and the LORD has granted your request."

1 SAMUEL 12:13 NLT

Have you ever received the exact thing you requested, only to immediately regret the request? Israel did. Samuel was old, and his children didn't follow in his footsteps, so the Israelites requested a king in place of a judge. After all, that's what all the other countries had.

But Israel already had a king. God was the King of Israel.

When you place your faith in human solutions—political leaders, money, or anything else that is not God—you are trusting in less than God has already given: Himself. He is the King of kings and Lord of lords!

When you follow after lesser kings, you will only succeed in going where they lead. If they lead you to the Lord, great! But why take the chance? Stop requesting kings when you already have one.

CLASSICS: CHARLES H. SPURGEON

JESUS IS GOD

And daily in the temple, and in every house, they ceased not to teach and preach Jesus Christ.

ACTS 5:42 KJV

They continued both to teach and preach Jesus Christ. To preach Jesus Christ aright we must preach Him in His infinite and indisputable Godhead. We may be attacked by philosophers, who will either make Him no God at all, or one constituted temporarily and, I must add, absurdly a God for a season. We shall have at once upon us those who view Christ as a prophet, as a great man, as an admirable exemplar; we shall be assailed on all sides by those who choose rather to draw their divinity from their own addled brains than from the simplicity of Holy Writ; but what mattereth this?

We must reiterate again and again the absolute and proper deity of Christ; for without this. . .soon will our enemies prevail against us. . . . If He were not God, He was the greatest deceiver that ever lived. But God He is; and here, in this house, we must and will adore Him.

GOD LOVES JEWS AND GENTILES ALIKE

The voice spoke to him a second time, "Do not call anything impure that God has made clean."

ACTS 10:15 NIV

Peter was born and raised a Jew. He followed laws and customs, and he knew others expected him to trust tradition. He took pride in doing his best to follow what his fellow countrymen followed.

Even after he received the Holy Spirit, Peter followed Jewish dietary laws—until the Lord appeared to him in a vision and told him to "kill and eat" animals Peter knew were forbidden. At first, Peter refused, telling God that he wouldn't eat anything that was unclean or impure. God's response? Reread today's scripture.

Food wasn't the point of what God did that day. He was teaching His apostle that Jesus had come as Savior for all mankind—not just the Jews. No longer should Peter—or anyone—see non-Jews as "unclean" or "impure." As the apostle Paul wrote, "There is neither Jew nor Gentile, neither slave nor free, nor is there male and female, for you are all one in Christ Jesus" (Galatians 3:28 NIV).

THE SPIRIT'S PRAYERS

Likewise the Spirit also helpeth our infirmities: for we know not what we should pray for as we ought: but the Spirit itself maketh intercession for us with groanings which cannot be uttered.

ROMANS 8:26 KJV

At times in life, prayer seems almost impossible. Pressure, frustration, and outright despair can muddle our minds to the point that there will be no coherent conversations with God.

Of course, since He is God, He knew these times would occur—and He made provision for them.

We know that God is a Trinity of Father, Son, and Spirit. By belief in the Son's work, we become members of the Father's family, sealed with the gift of the Spirit. And the Spirit, who is actually God living inside us, prays to the Father on our behalf.

What a God we serve! He makes the effort to provide salvation for us, draw us to Himself, seal us with His Spirit, and then pray for us when we struggle. And you can be sure that the Spirit's prayers are effective ones.

GOD SEES WHAT'S WITHIN

But the Lord said to Samuel, "Do not consider his appearance or his height, for I have rejected him. The Lord does not look at the things people look at. People look at the outward appearance, but the Lord looks at the heart."

1 SAMUEL 16:7 NIV

There are some things you can tell about a man just by looking at him. You can tell about how tall he is, what clothes he wears, and what he looks like. But there are many more things you can't determine by appearance alone.

When we make judgments about people based on their appearance, we infringe upon the domain of God. God alone knows what is going on in a person's head and heart. Since we are not privy to those areas of a person's life, it should not be up to us to decide whom to love and whom to reject.

It is God's job to determine justice. It is our job to love others as He has loved us.

CLASSICS: D. L. MOODY

FAITH IS THE GOLDEN KEY

David said moreover, The Lord that delivered me out of the paw of the lion, and out of the paw of the bear, he will deliver me out of the hand of this Philistine. And Saul said unto David, Go, and the Lord be with thee.

1 SAMUEL 17:37 KJV

We are not told that Jesus ever taught His disciples how to preach, but He taught them how to pray. He wanted them to have power with God; then He knew they would have power with man. In James we read: "If any of you lack wisdom, let him ask of God. . .and it shall be given him; but let him ask in faith, nothing wavering." So faith is the golden key that unlocks the treasures of heaven.

It was the shield that David took when he met Goliath on the field; he believed that God was going to deliver the Philistine into his hands. Someone has said that faith could lead Christ about anywhere; wherever He found it He honored it. Unbelief sees something in God's hand and says, "I cannot get it." Faith sees it and says, "I will have it."

WE BEAR JESUS' NAME

*It was at Antioch that the believers
were first called Christians.*

ACTS 11:26 NLT

In case there's any question, "Christ" isn't Jesus' last name. It's a title indicating that He is the Messiah, the Anointed One of God, the Savior of the world. But the title is so much a part of Jesus' life and work that it's essentially a name. And it's a name that we, as His followers, bear in the world.

The book of Acts is the story of the early church, of the spread of Christianity after the death, resurrection, and ascension of Jesus. As persecution scattered believers from Jerusalem and Judea, the Gospel took root in "the uttermost part of the earth" (Acts 1:8 KJV), as Jesus had predicted. In one of those places, Antioch of Syria, the believers became known as "Christians," clearly distinguishing them as belonging to Jesus.

The name has endured through two millennia and encompasses all of us today who believe in the person and message of the Lord. You bear Jesus' name in the world—wear it well!

GOD'S AMAZING LOVE

This is love: not that we loved God, but that he loved us and sent his Son as an atoning sacrifice for our sins. Dear friends, since God so loved us, we also ought to love one another.

1 JOHN 4:10–11 NIV

Each of the apostles, to his dying day, was renowned for his intimate walk with God, his passion for unity in the church, and his sacrificial love for others. What compelled each of these men to give the rest of their lives, year after year, decade after decade, to the Lord's service?

Beyond the example of the apostles, our attention is drawn back to the amazing, intimate, sacrificial love that God the Father and Jesus have demonstrated to us and to the rest of the world.

The apostle John, the closest friend of Jesus during His time on earth, couldn't get over that divine love. Reread today's scripture, think it over, even commit it to memory. It is basic to your Christian life—and a great encouragement in times of trouble.

GOD IS WAITING FOR YOU

But in their distress they turned to the LORD, the God of Israel, and sought him, and he was found by them.

2 CHRONICLES 15:4 NIV

If you're at all familiar with Old Testament history, you know that the nation of Israel—God's chosen people—often failed. In fact, the people and their leaders were so troubled that Israel split into competing nations, a northern kingdom (still called Israel) and a southern kingdom (Judah). They squabbled for generations before each was carried off by foreign powers.

The story of God's people is generally dreary. . .but there are glimmers of hope, as in today's scripture. This was the word of the prophet Oded to Judah's king Asa. Though the nation's sins had led to God "troubling them with every kind of distress" (verse 6 NIV), Oded told Asa, "Be strong and do not give up, for your work will be rewarded" (verse 7 NIV).

No matter where you've been and what you've done, God waits for you too. Turn His way.

CLASSICS: D. L. MOODY

GOD KEEPS HIS PROMISES

In hope of eternal life, which God, that cannot lie, promised . . .
TITUS 1:2–3 KJV

God is always true to what He promises to do. He made promises to Abraham, Jacob, Moses, Joshua, etc., and did He not fulfill them? He will fulfill every word of what He has promised; yet how few take Him at His word!

When I was a young man I was clerk in the establishment of a man in Chicago, whom I observed frequently occupied sorting and marking bills. He explained to me what he had been doing; on some notes he had marked B, on some D, and on others G; those marked B he told me were bad, those marked D meant they were doubtful, and those with G on them meant they were good; and, said he, you must treat all of them accordingly. And thus people endorse God's promises, by marking some as bad and others as doubtful; whereas we ought to take all of them as good, for He has never once broken His word, and all that He says He will do, will be done in the fulness of time.

THE ANCIENT OF DAYS

*"As I looked, thrones were set in place,
and the Ancient of Days took his seat."*

DANIEL 7:9 NIV

Three times, Daniel describes God as the "Ancient of Days." The name is descriptive enough to contribute to our understanding of God yet nebulous enough to deepen the mysteries of His nature.

The phrase strikes a host of chords at once. It signifies God's eternal nature—His persistence through time immeasurable. But it also hints at something more undefinable: His *otherness*. God's existence is too concrete to be labeled as a mere idea, yet He dwells in a plane of reality that words can never hope to reach. He sits beyond the threads of time and space, witnessing the future and the past as though they were one.

While God has revealed some aspects of His ancient, mysterious nature through His Word, we can only glimpse these truths "through a glass, darkly"; one day, however, we will see Him "face to face" (1 Corinthians 13:12 KJV).

GOD'S UNDESERVED GRACE

"We believe that we are all saved the same way,
by the undeserved grace of the Lord Jesus."

ACTS 15:11 NLT

In today's world, people believe many things about what it takes to be saved and enter heaven. Some think that if you do more good things than bad, God will let you into His presence for eternity. Others say that if you go to church and are nice to others, you're in. Still others believe that if they dedicate their lives to feeding the poor and rescuing the exploited, they will receive the eternal reward.

For the first-century church, the way to salvation was simple. They recognized that all people are rescued the same way—by God's grace offered to the undeserving. Jesus our Savior made a stunning offer: a place in heaven with Him and His family both for the worst of sinners and the nicest people alike. There's no need to clean up before you ask for His gift of rescue. God's grace makes it possible to receive what you don't deserve—forgiveness, love, and adoption into His eternal family.

GOD HATES HUMAN PRIDE

Now there was no one in Israel as good looking and as much praised as Absalom. There was nothing wrong with him from the bottom of his foot to the top of his head. At the end of every year he would cut the hair from his head, for it was heavy on him. When he cut it, he weighed the hair of his head. It weighed as much as 200 pieces of silver, by the king's weight.

2 SAMUEL 14:25–26 NLV

Absalom was ridiculously handsome and had luxurious hair. In his pride, he usurped his father David's authority and rebelled. As public opinion shifted toward Absalom, David left town.

But the story didn't end there.

While he was out riding his horse one day, Absalom's mane of hair got tangled in the branches of an oak tree, and his horse rode right out from under him. Absalom was soon surrounded by supporters of David and died while suspended from the tree limb (see 2 Samuel 18:9).

To avoid a hairy end, remember that God hates human pride. He will never reward it.

CLASSICS: CHARLES H. SPURGEON

LOOK TO THE CREATOR, NOT THE CREATURE

And the LORD said unto Moses, Is the LORD's hand waxed short? thou shalt see now whether my word shall come to pass unto thee or not.

NUMBERS 11:23 KJV

God had made a positive promise to Moses that for the space of a whole month He would feed the vast host in the wilderness with flesh. Moses, being overtaken by a fit of unbelief, looks to the outward means, calculates his commissariat and is at a loss to know how the promise can be fulfilled. Shall the flocks and the herds be slain? . . . Shall all the fish of the sea leave their watery element and come to the tables of these clamorous hungry men? Even then, Moses thought there would be scarcely food enough to feed so vast a host for a month. You will see, my brethren, right readily the mistake which Moses made. He looked to the creature instead of the Creator. Doth the Creator expect the creature to fulfill His promise? No; He that makes fulfills. If He speaks, it is done—done by Himself.

GOD'S TRUTH

*I have no greater joy than to hear that
my children are walking in the truth.*

3 JOHN 4 NIV

The apostle John had heard some good reports about a Christian man named Gaius—namely, that he was "walking in truth"—and in today's scripture, he celebrated what he'd heard with his readers.

In the Bible, the words *walk* or *walking* often refer simply to how a man lives. But "What is truth?" to quote an important Bible character, Pontius Pilate (John 18:38 NIV). Jesus answered that question on the night He was arrested, when He prayed to His heavenly Father for the apostles: "Sanctify them by the truth; your word is truth" (John 17:17 NIV).

God is the ultimate source of truth, and He has revealed that truth in His written Word, the Bible. So learn His truth by reading and studying His Word. But don't just learn about it—live it out every day.

BY GOD'S SPIRIT

So he said to me, "This is the word of the Lord to Zerubbabel: 'Not by might nor by power, but by my Spirit,' says the Lord Almighty."

ZECHARIAH 4:6 NIV

Zerubbabel was tasked with rebuilding Solomon's temple following the Jews' return from exile in Babylon. With the help of Joshua, the high priest, he began to rebuild what the Babylonians had destroyed.

This task would ultimately take more than twenty years, and it did not go smoothly or easily. Seemingly friendly offers of assistance masked hostility. Opposition to the project caused the King of Persia to withdraw his support, leading to a delay of nearly seventeen years.

But in the midst of these challenges, Zerubbabel kept his eyes on the God who promised to empower him and his people through His own Holy Spirit.

God offers us the very same thing today. As we face the tasks of our lives, let's walk in God's promise to Zerubbabel and proclaim, "Not by my own might or power, but by the Spirit of God!"

THE GIFT OF GOD'S WORD

They received the message with great eagerness and examined the Scriptures every day to see if what Paul said was true.

ACTS 17:11 NIV

Today's scripture describes a group of first-century Jewish believers who practiced due diligence. They studied the scriptures to affirm what the apostle Paul had told them. These people were determined not to be led astray, so they went straight to the Bible to make sure that didn't happen.

God lovingly gave us the gift of His written Word—the Bible—so that we can read it, study it. . .and prove (or disprove) the things we hear about Him from others. God wants you to learn about Him from Bible-based teaching and preaching—that's why He gives pastors and teachers to the world. But each of us should want to go to the Bible ourselves to see what God has actually said.

Imagine, the all-powerful Creator and Sustainer of the universe providing a written record of Himself to His own. What love that demonstrates!

CLASSICS: D. L. MOODY

GOD BEARS LONG WITH MEN

And account that the longsuffering of our Lord is salvation.

2 PETER 3:15 KJV

Why are His chariots so long in coming? Why does He delay? The world grows grey, not alone with age, but with iniquity; and yet the Deliverer comes not. We have waited for His footfall at the dead of night and looked out for Him through the gates of the morning and expected Him in the heat of the day and reckoned that He might come ere yet another sun went down; but He is not here! He waits. He waits very, very long. Will He not come?

Longsuffering is that which keeps Him from coming. He is bearing with men. Not yet the thunderbolt! Not yet the riven heavens and the reeling earth! Not yet the great white throne and the day of judgment; for He is very pitiful and beareth long with men!

GOD LISTENS

*In my distress I called upon the Lord, and cried
to my God: and he did hear my voice out of his
temple, and my cry did enter into his ears.*

2 SAMUEL 22:7 KJV

There are billions of people in the world, each with needs as unique as themselves. And yet, God cares about each one of us. He is not overwhelmed by the numbers or needs of His people. He cares about the big stuff and the small.

Like a doting parent, God wants to hear all about your day, your concerns, your interests, your struggles, and your victories. God is listening for your cries, ready to comfort you with His love.

When was the last time you had a heart-to-heart conversation with your Creator? Yes, He knows what you will say before you say it, but he wants the relationship that comes with communication.

GOD'S PROMISE THROUGH JUDE

To him who is able to keep you from stumbling and to present you before his glorious presence without fault and with great joy—to the only God our Savior be glory, majesty, power and authority, through Jesus Christ our Lord, before all ages, now and forevermore! Amen.

JUDE 24–25 NIV

In Jude 20–23, the half-brother of Jesus urges us to follow his own real-life example. First, Jude built himself up in the most holy Christian faith. Second, he prayed in the Holy Spirit. Third, he kept himself in God's love. Fourth, he waited for the mercy of the Lord Jesus Christ to bring him to eternal life. Fifth, he was merciful to those who doubted. Sixth, he saved others by snatching them from the fire, showing mercy mixed with fear—hating the repugnant flesh, world, and devil.

If we do these things, Jude offers us the wonderful promise in today's scripture. Be sure to grab hold of that promise every "today."

AMAZING GRACE

"Now, my brothers, I give you over to God and to the word of His love. It is able to make you strong."

ACTS 20:32 NLV

After spending three years giving of himself to the Ephesian Christians, Paul shared the words of farewell recorded in Acts 20:18-38. In today's scripture, he spoke confidently of the Ephesians' source of strength going forward: God's promise of grace, meaning His unmerited favor upon them.

In his epistles, Paul wrote much of God's grace. He said that we are saved by grace through faith, that we are sustained in our faith through God's grace, that we are strengthened as a result of God's grace. Now, as he bid the Ephesians farewell, Paul assured them that God's grace would keep them during the difficult days ahead.

This message wasn't just for the Ephesians. God's amazing grace applies to every believer of all time. . . including you today.

CLASSICS: D. L. MOODY

JESUS IS WORTHY OF YOUR WORSHIP

Worthy is the Lamb.

REVELATION 5:12 KJV

We have got on record what heaven thinks of Christ. Here on earth He was not known—no one seemed really to understand Him; but He was known in that world in which He had been from the very foundation thereof; for He was there before the morning stars sang together, before Adam was placed in this world. We are told that John was in the Spirit on the Lord's day, and being caught up, he heard a loud shout around him, and looking, he saw ten thousand times ten thousand angels, who were shouting, "Worthy is the Lamb that was slain, to receive power, and riches, and wisdom, and strength, and honor, and glory, and blessing!"

Yes, Jesus is worthy of all this. That is what heaven thinks of Him; would that earth also would take up the echo and join with heaven in singing, "He is worthy to receive power, and riches, and wisdom, and strength, and honor, and glory, and blessing!"

GOD IS WORTHY OF ALL WORSHIP

*"You are worthy, our Lord and God, to receive glory
and honor and power, for you created all things, and
by your will they were created and have their being."*

REVELATION 4:11 NIV

In Revelation 4–5, the apostle John, who said he was "in the Spirit" (4:2), tells us what heaven looks and sounds like.

The chapter after today's scripture, John makes the provocative statement that he saw "every creature in heaven and on earth and under the earth and on the sea, and all that is in them" and heard them sing: "To him who sits on the throne and to the Lamb be praise and honor and glory and power, for ever and ever!" (Revelation 5:13 NIV).

In other words, while "in the Spirit," John saw and heard "every creature" (including himself) worshipping God. What an amazing thought! Perhaps we should memorize these songs of Revelation. After all, along with "every creature," we'll someday be singing them to God!

GOD GIVES SPIRITUAL LIFE

*The Lord heard Elijah's cry, and the boy's life returned
to him, and he lived. Elijah picked up the child and carried
him down from the room into the house. He gave him
to his mother and said, "Look, your son is alive!"*

1 KINGS 17:22–23 NIV

There are only a few instances where God allows the
dead to be brought back to life, at least in the physical
sense. And while physical life *is* great, it is still tem-
porary. The people the prophets restored to physical
life ended up dying again.

Fortunately, God is not only interested in physical
well-being. He is the giver and sustainer of spiritual life.
When Jesus rose from the grave, He made it possible for
those who believe in Him to have eternal spiritual life.

You may be alive physically, but are you alive spiritually as well? If not, God is waiting to hear your cry
and bestow the spiritual life you've been waiting for.
When you have it, the angels will rejoice and echo
Elijah from today's scripture: "Look, your son is alive!"

CREATION INVITES YOU TO NOTICE GOD

Ever since the world was created, people have seen the earth and sky. Through everything God made, they can clearly see his invisible qualities—his eternal power and divine nature. So they have no excuse for not knowing God.

ROMANS 1:20 NLT

God is "hiding" in plain sight. His creation invites you to notice Him.

Of course, as Christians, we recognize this truth. Our complex world of trees and birds and water and light could not have come into being by itself. Only an all-knowing, all-powerful God could have made such a world, so perfectly balanced for life. And only an infinite God could have envisioned and executed the vast reaches of space, populated by countless heavenly bodies.

Some people try hard to dismiss the witness of the earth and sky, the unambiguous statement of God's "eternal power and divine nature." They have no excuse for doing so, and in His mercy, God gives them time to acknowledge Him. For those of us who already know Him, let's just marvel at the amazing world He's made. He's given us "everything for our enjoyment" (1 Timothy 6:17 NIV).

GOD STIRS US TO DO GOOD

*Now in the first year of Cyrus king of Persia, that the word
of the Lord by the mouth of Jeremiah might be fulfilled,
the Lord stirred up the spirit of Cyrus king of Persia, that
he made a proclamation throughout all his kingdom.*

EZRA 1:1 KJV

The Lord stirred up the spirit of Cyrus. The hearts of
kings are in the hand of the Lord, and, like the rivulets
of water, He turneth them which way soever He will. It
is said of Cyrus that he knew not God nor how to serve
Him, but God knew him and how to serve Himself by
him (Isaiah 45:4).

God governs the world by His influence on the
spirits of men, and, whatever good is done at any time,
it is God that stirs up the spirit to do it, puts thoughts
into the mind, gives to the understanding to form a
right judgment and directs the will which way He
pleases. Whatever good offices therefore are, at any
time, done for the church of God, He must have the
glory of them.

POWER IN GOD'S WORD

For the word of God is alive and active. Sharper than any double-edged sword, it penetrates even to dividing soul and spirit, joints and marrow; it judges the thoughts and attitudes of the heart.

HEBREWS 4:12 NIV

Certain aspects of God's character can be understood through creation. His wisdom and power shine through space, our earth, and the countless living creatures we see. Human beings, reflecting His image, hint at His ability to communicate and love. All of these things, the apostle Paul said, leave people who dismiss God "without excuse" (Romans 1:20 NIV).

For the fullest possible picture, though, we need a definitive revelation, which God has provided in His Word. By scripture, we learn God's names, the breadth of His characteristics, the problem of human sin, and the solution: Jesus Christ. God's Word, the Bible, provides everything we need for life on this earth and throughout eternity. . .because it is a living, breathing part of Him.

Why not devote some additional time to His Word today?

OUR HUMBLE KING

Rejoice greatly, Daughter Zion! Shout, Daughter Jerusalem! See, your king comes to you, righteous and victorious, lowly and riding on a donkey, on a colt, the foal of a donkey.

ZECHARIAH 9:9 NIV

During His time on earth, Jesus perfectly exhibited a character quality His Father in heaven valued greatly: humility. From the moment of His birth in a Bethlehem stable to His death on a cross—a death reserved for violent criminals—Jesus was a picture of humility achieved by no other person before or since.

Today's scripture verse is an Old Testament prophecy concerning an event called the "Triumphal Entry"—when Jesus made His final entry into Jerusalem riding not on a powerful white steed but on the back of a lowly donkey colt.

This kind of humility was essential to who Jesus was. . .and to His willingness to provide for our salvation when He "humbled himself by becoming obedient to death—even death on a cross!" (Philippians 2:8 NIV).

THE JEALOUS GOD

Then the Lord will be jealous for
His land and have pity on His people.

JOEL 2:18 NLV

For humans, jealousy can be sinful—a flaw that has led to the downfall of many. However, as Exodus 34:14 (KJV) says, "The LORD, whose name is Jealous, is a jealous God."

We shouldn't presume that God has a double standard; the difference between us and Him is that He alone is worthy of all praise, and we are not. He is the only Being in the universe who has a right to jealousy.

In Joel's description of God, an even deeper truth emerges: God is not jealous only for His own honor—He's jealous for His people. For *us*.

Just as He chose Israel and fought vehemently on their side whenever they began living for Him, He now chooses those who trust in Jesus, His Son, and He will fight for them until the end of time.

God, the King of the universe, is jealous for you. Are you living for Him?

CLASSICS: CHARLES H. SPURGEON

THE ANSWER TO ALL DOUBT AND FEAR

Though he slay me, yet will I trust in him: but I will maintain mine own ways before him.

JOB 13:15 KJV

This is one of the supreme sayings of scripture. It rises, like an alpine summit, clear above all ordinary heights of speech; it pierces the clouds and glistens in the light of God. If I were required to quote a selection of the sublimest utterances of the human mind, I should mention this among the first: "Though he slay me, yet will I trust in him."

Methinks I might almost say to the man who thus spoke what our Lord said to Simon Peter when he had declared Him to be the Son of the Highest: "Flesh and blood hath not revealed this unto thee." . . . It is well worthy of observation that in these words Job answered both the accusations of Satan and the charges of his friends.

GOD'S KINDNESS LEADS TO REPENTANCE

Do you show contempt for the riches of his kindness, forbearance and patience, not realizing that God's kindness is intended to lead you to repentance?

ROMANS 2:4 NIV

We tend to think of the Lord as an all-loving, all-patient, and all-kind God—and those things are certainly true. However, too many of us don't fully understand what His kindness really means. Many Christian men today tend to think of God as a friend who loves you so much that He will turn a blind eye to sin.

The scripture above is clear that God's kindness serves a very different purpose. In His kindness, He patiently waits for men to recognize their sin and turn away from it—that is repentance—so they can begin a new journey with Him. This journey will lead us safely through the hardships and pitfalls of this world into His eternal presence. God's kindness leads us to repentance.

WHEN GOD SHOWS UP

About noontime Elijah began mocking them. "You'll have to shout louder," he scoffed, "for surely he is a god! Perhaps he is daydreaming, or is relieving himself. Or maybe he is away on a trip, or is asleep and needs to be wakened!"

1 KINGS 18:27 NLT

In the epic showdown on Mount Carmel (1 Kings 18:20–40), the prophets of Baal spent hours trying to get Baal to light their altar and accept their sacrifice. While they danced and cut themselves to please their god, Elijah scoffed.

When it was his turn to call on God, Elijah doused his altar three times with water and said a simple prayer. God showed up. Fire came from heaven and consumed the sacrifice, the altar, and every drop of water.

God is unlimited in His power. He can make a blazing inferno from the soggy mess of our lives if only we will pray and dedicate ourselves to Him. Are you ready to be on fire for the Lord?

GOD IS EVERYTHING WE ARE NOT

God is always true even if every man lies. The Holy Writings say, "Speak the truth and you will not be proven guilty."

ROMANS 3:4 NLV

It may sound harsh, but it must be said: God is everything we're not. He's faithful when we let others down. He loves when we refuse. He tells the truth while lies slip from our mouths.

Think about it: If God were to be anything less than He is, if He weren't the absolute standard of truth and righteousness, then He wouldn't set a standard of *better* for you to follow. But He sets the standard of truth and truthfulness perfectly and invites you to embrace it as well.

God will never consider as guilty the man committed to speaking the truth like He does, loving like He does, and living in faithfulness like He does. Even when we fail, our perfect God offers perfect forgiveness.

CLASSICS: CHARLES H. SPURGEON

GOD'S MERCY, LOVE, AND PUNISHMENT OF THE WICKED

If he turn not, he will whet his sword;
he hath bent his bow, and made it ready.

PSALM 7:12 KJV

If we dare to tell men that God will punish them for their sins, it is charged upon us that we want to bully them into religion, and if we faithfully and honestly tell our hearers that sin must bring after it certain destruction, it is said that we are attempting to frighten them into goodness. Now we care not what men mockingly impute to us; we feel it our duty, when men sin, to tell them they shall be punished, and so long as the world will not give up its sin we feel we must not cease our warnings.

But the cry of the age is, that God is merciful, that God is love. Ay; who said He was not? But remember, it is equally true, God is just, severely and inflexibly just. He were not God if He were not just; He could not be merciful if He were not just, for punishment of the wicked is demanded by the highest mercy to the rest of mankind.

JESUS WILL APPEAR!

Then I saw heaven opened, and a white horse was standing there. Its rider [Jesus Christ] was named Faithful and True, for he judges fairly and wages a righteous war.

REVELATION 19:11 NLT

Scripture consistently tells us God can appear in any form He chooses and to anyone He chooses. First, He appeared to some Old Testament believers like Abraham, Jacob, and Moses. Second, God appeared to His people during the Exodus from Egypt. Third, God's Son, Jesus Christ, became human and lived here on earth for more than thirty years. Fourth, Jesus repeatedly appeared to His disciples after His resurrection from the dead. Finally, our victorious Lord Jesus will appear once more at the climax of history as taught in Matthew 24:30, 2 Thessalonians 1:7, 2 Timothy 4:1, 2 Peter 1:19, and today's scripture.

That day is coming, with rewards for Jesus' faithful followers. Be encouraged. . .and be ready.

JESUS MAKES US RIGHTEOUS

Consequently, just as one trespass resulted in condemnation for all people, so also one righteous act resulted in justification and life for all people. For just as through the disobedience of the one man the many were made sinners, so also through the obedience of the one man the many will be made righteous.

ROMANS 5:18–19 NIV

Genesis 3 tells the tragic story of disobedience in the first two people—Adam and Eve—and God's pronouncement of judgment on all of humanity. Since then, all of us are born sinners in need of a Savior.

Today's scripture contrasts two men—Adam, whose disobedience resulted in the condemnation of all humankind, and Jesus Christ, whose obedience to His Father in heaven made many righteous before God.

In an act of unimaginable love, compassion, and grace, Jesus died for us while we were still sinners (see Romans 5:8) and was raised from the dead so that we could walk in the "abundant life" He promised those who follow Him.

We cannot make ourselves righteous. We can only accept the free gift Jesus offers. Why would anyone say no?

GOD WILL JUDGE

Then I saw a great white throne and him who was seated on it. The earth and the heavens fled from his presence, and there was no place for them. And I saw the dead, great and small, standing before the throne, and books were opened. Another book was opened, which is the book of life. The dead were judged according to what they had done as recorded in the books.

REVELATION 20:11–12 NIV

Today's scripture—as well as Matthew 25:31–32 and Matthew 25:41–46—point to a time at the end of human history when all people will appear before the Lord for judgment according to their works here on earth. And lest we mistakenly think we earn salvation by our good deeds, Jesus Himself said, "The work of God is this: to believe in the one he has sent" (John 6:29 NIV).

Because God is holy, He must—and will—judge sin. We who have accepted His offer of forgiveness through faith in Jesus must now pray earnestly for our not-yet-saved loved ones.

CLASSICS: CHARLES H. SPURGEON

OUR GOD RESTORES US

*He restoreth my soul: he leadeth me in the paths
of righteousness for his name's sake.*

PSALM 23:3 KJV

The poet laureate of scripture sings surpassingly in this psalm, and every line is dedicated to the Beloved of his soul, in whom were all his fresh springs. My object while handling a part of one of his verses shall be the same as his own; I also would speak of "things which I have made touching the King," with the view of extolling His name. I desire to glorify Him from one particular point of view, namely, as the Restorer, who His own self brings back our wandering spirits when we forsake His ways.

I would just now write the first word of the text in capitals, capitals as large as you can find. "HE restoreth my soul." He, He alone, He and not another. Unto Him be praise!

THE GOD WHO FREES US

Don't you know that when you offer yourselves to someone as obedient slaves, you are slaves of the one you obey—whether you are slaves to sin, which leads to death, or to obedience, which leads to righteousness? But thanks be to God that, though you used to be slaves to sin, you have come to obey from your heart the pattern of teaching that has now claimed your allegiance.

ROMANS 6:16–17 NIV

God loves giving His people freedom. He freed His beloved people, the ancient Hebrews, from lives of slavery in Egypt, and several centuries later freed them again from the captivity that began under Babylon.

Today, God graciously offers us another kind of freedom—from our slavery to sin.

Today's scripture indicates that we have but two choices: slavery to sin or slavery to obedience, which "leads to righteousness." The apostle Paul expressed his gratitude to God that we as believers are no longer slaves to sin—that we can choose from our hearts to live in obedience to our Lord.

That is what true faith and freedom in Jesus are all about!

PROVE GOD

Prove me now herewith, saith the Lord of hosts, if I will not open you the windows of heaven, and pour you out a blessing, that there shall not be room enough to receive it.

MALACHI 3:10 KJV

Perhaps we've seen people misuse a scripture like today's, giving in order to get, trying to manipulate God into "paying back" an offering—with plenty of interest. But beware of assuming that a poor example makes these words—*God's words*—untrue:

"Will a mere mortal rob God? Yet you rob me. But you ask, 'How are we robbing you?' In tithes and offerings. You are under a curse—your whole nation—because you are robbing me. Bring the whole tithe into the storehouse, that there may be food in my house. Test me in this," says the LORD *Almighty, "and see if I will not throw open the floodgates of heaven and pour out so much blessing that there will not be room enough to store it."*

MALACHI 3:8–10 NIV

Skeptical? Prove God. Trust Him and see if He will not pour out so much blessing you won't have enough room to receive it.

GOD CARES ABOUT LITTLE THINGS

As one of them was cutting down a tree, the iron axhead fell into the water. "Oh no, my lord!" he cried out. "It was borrowed!" The man of God asked, "Where did it fall?" When he showed him the place, Elisha cut a stick and threw it there, and made the iron float.

2 KINGS 6:5–6 NIV

Some people believe that as Creator and Sustainer of the universe, God is too busy for the little things. Sure, He's the One you pray to when your health takes a dive or when your home is destroyed by a tornado—but does God really care about your lost car keys?

Actually, He does.

When an acquaintance of Elisha lost the head of a borrowed ax in the Jordan River, the man of God helped him, demonstrating that God cares about all things, great and small. Often, God will use one of His children to help another.

Today, look for an opportunity to help someone in need. It doesn't have to be a life-threatening emergency. Simply help out, and you'll be doing God's work.

CLASSICS: CHARLES H. SPURGEON

WHEN NOTHING ELSE IS LEFT, GOD REMAINS

For the LORD is our judge, the LORD is our lawgiver, the LORD is our king; he will save us. . . . And the inhabitant shall not say, I am sick: the people that dwell therein shall be forgiven their iniquity.

ISAIAH 33:22, 24 KJV

When the worst had come to the worst, He laid bare His arm and brought deliverance for His people. Is not this a general rule with God? Is it not a truth fraught with comfort to any of you whose day has darkened down into a sevenfold midnight? When nothing else is left your God remains and God appears. When all your own strength fails you, your strength shall be to sit still while God arises and becomes your arm every morning, your salvation in the time of trouble. I would encourage all who are in spiritual distress to gather hope from this chapter, since it is addressed to Zion in her sore affliction.

OUR HEAVENLY FATHER

For those who are led by the Spirit of God are the children of God. The Spirit you received does not make you slaves, so that you live in fear again; rather, the Spirit you received brought about your adoption to sonship. And by him we cry, "Abba, Father."

ROMANS 8:14–15 NIV

In the four Gospels, Jesus referred many times to God as "My Father." Not only that, God openly proclaimed His relationship to Jesus when He spoke from heaven, "This is my Son, whom I love; with him I am well pleased" (Matthew 3:17 NIV).

God the Father and Jesus the Son have shared a wonderfully close, intimate relationship from eternity past, one that will continue into eternity future. As human beings, we have no eternity past—but we will get to enjoy that future relationship with God forever.

Through Jesus, you have the privilege of living in an intimate, joyful relationship with God—a relationship so close that you can call Him what Jesus did: "Abba, Father!"

GOD'S NEW ORDER

"'He will wipe every tear from their eyes. There will be no more death' or mourning or crying or pain, for the old order of things has passed away."

REVELATION 21:4 NIV

Since the fall of humanity in the garden of Eden, people have felt the terrible effects of sin. Death, loss, grief, and suffering have all become an agonizing, persistent part of the human condition. But God had a plan to put an end to what sin has done to His most prized creation.

Because of His great love and the healing work of Jesus on the cross, a day will come when grief and suffering and sorrow are no more. Instead, we will all walk in newness of life—the free gift of a supremely loving God.

Through the New Testament, Jesus Christ and His apostles repeatedly urged all Christians to look forward to that first day of eternity, when we all take up residence in a place God calls the New Jerusalem. It's coming. . .and it's going to be glorious.

GOD'S PLEASURES

You make known to me the path of life; you will fill me with joy in your presence, with eternal pleasures at your right hand.

PSALM 16:11 NIV

We enjoy many pleasures in this life: family and friends, food and drink, pets and cars and travel and entertainment. But as good as many of these things are, none lasts forever.

God, though, has planned "eternal pleasures" for His people. What exactly that means remains to be seen, but we know that a day is coming when "there will be no more death or mourning or crying or pain, for the old order of things has passed away" (Revelation 21:4 NIV). In fact, everything will be new—and God's "new" will be absolute perfection.

Whether we look forward to reunions with loved ones, feasting with the saints of old, or exploring a universe without any remaining stain of sin, let's be sure to remember the ultimate pleasure of eternity: the intimate and ongoing presence of God Himself.

CLASSICS: JOHN WESLEY

OUR ETERNAL GOD

Before the mountains were brought forth, or ever thou hadst formed the earth and the world, even from everlasting to everlasting, thou art God.

PSALM 90:2 KJV

Eternity has generally been considered as divisible into two parts, which have been termed, in plain English, that eternity which is past and that eternity which is to come. And does there not seem to be an intimation of this distinction in the text? "Thou art God from everlasting"—here is an expression of that eternity which is past. "To everlasting"—here is an expression of that eternity which is to come. Perhaps, indeed, some may think it is not strictly proper to say there is an eternity that is past. But the meaning is easily understood: We mean thereby duration which had no beginning; as by eternity to come, we mean that duration which will have no end.

It is God alone who (to use the exalted language of scripture) "inhabiteth eternity" in both these senses. The great Creator alone (not any of His creatures) is "from everlasting to everlasting": His duration alone, as it had no beginning, so it cannot have any end.

THE GOD OF ULTIMATE WISDOM

Shall I not in that day, saith the Lord, even destroy the wise men out of Edom, and understanding out of the mount of Esau?

OBADIAH 8 KJV

As the book of Proverbs attests, wisdom is a valuable asset for God's people. It teaches us deep truths about God's love and guides our footsteps into His will for our lives.

There's another type of wisdom, however, one that originates not from God but from the human mind. Instead of learning from divine revelation, this wisdom attempts to dethrone God's truth with the very mind that God Himself created.

When Jesus returns, Obadiah's warning against this type of wisdom will find its deepest fulfillment. Even the wisest philosophers will kneel, speechless in the presence of God's holiness.

But until that day, we must continue to trust Him, waging spiritual war against those who seek to destroy God's Word. By devoting our minds to discovering God's truth, we will stand firm in the wisdom that only He provides.

A GOD OF TRANSFORMATION

Don't copy the behavior and customs of this world, but let God transform you into a new person by changing the way you think.

ROMANS 12:2 NLT

A man who follows Jesus faithfully—a man who has God's Holy Spirit living inside him—is a man who wouldn't continue in the world's thinking and behavior, both of which oppose our Father in heaven. Instead, the true Christian man lives and thinks in ways that God has indicated are pleasing to Him.

The keyword of today's scripture is *transform*. It tells us how God, through His Spirit, enables us to avoid living like the world and instead live in the way He wants.

God never saves us to leave us as we were. Instead, He works within us for transformation—of our behavior, our speech, and our thoughts. Our part in this transformation is simple: just let Him!

STRENGTH AND SAFETY
IN GOD'S HANDS

Satan rose up against Israel and caused David to take a census of the people of Israel. So David said to Joab and the commanders of the army, "Take a census of all the people of Israel—from Beersheba in the south to Dan in the north—and bring me a report so I may know how many there are."

1 CHRONICLES 21:1–2 NLT

An accurate census is necessary for governments to run efficiently. There's nothing inherently evil about it. But today's passage refers to something other than typical government tallies. David was apparently measuring the strength of his nation by the people living there rather than by the living God they served.

Numbers—be it the size of an army or how many people you can influence—don't matter when pitted against the strength of God. Don't judge your strength or safety by numbers. Place your strength and safety back in God's hands, where they belong.

CLASSICS: ANDREW MURRAY

WAIT FOR GOD'S COUNSEL

They soon forgat his works; they waited not for his counsel.

PSALM 106:13 KJV

Our whole relation to God is ruled in this, that His will is to be done in us and by us as it is in heaven. He has promised to make known His will to us by His Spirit, the Guide into all truth. And our position is to be that of waiting for His counsel as the only guide of our thoughts and actions.

In our church worship, in our prayer meetings, in our conventions, in all our gatherings as managers, or directors, or committees, or helpers in any part of the work for God, our first object ought ever to be to ascertain the mind of God. God always works according to the counsel of His will; the more that counsel of His will is sought and found and honored, the more surely and mightily will God do His work for us and through us.

A VISION OF JESUS' ETERNAL KINGDOM

He who is the faithful witness to all these things says, "Yes, I am coming soon!" Amen! Come, Lord Jesus! May the grace of the Lord Jesus be with God's holy people.

REVELATION 22:20–21 NLT

Revelation is the New Testament's only book of prophecy. It is an apocalyptic vision of the future. As such, Revelation deliberately weaves in many themes from the book of Genesis to portray paradise restored after God's wrath is fully revealed against Satan, death, and sin. It also masterfully weaves in many other themes from the Old and New Testaments.

In several remarkable passages, especially the closing chapters, Revelation clearly and compellingly presents a vision of Jesus Christ's future kingdom and the new heavens, new earth, and new Jerusalem. What dynamic, thrilling rewards, opportunities, and experiences await us.

Once you read Revelation, you'll be tempted to go back and begin reading the Bible all over again. That's not a bad idea at all. Why not start with the new year?

YOU PLUS GOD EQUALS VICTORY

"The Lord has driven out before you great and powerful nations; to this day no one has been able to withstand you. One of you routs a thousand, because the Lord your God fights for you, just as he promised. So be very careful to love the Lord your God."

JOSHUA 23:9–11 NIV

Our God is jealous for His own (Joel 2:18), a powerful warrior (Exodus 15:3), and ready to fight for His people (Deuteronomy 1:30). Today's scripture indicates that there is one element essential to His success: you.

During Joshua's farewell address to the elders of Israel, the man who led God's people into the promised land said that they were successful because God fought *for* and, more specifically, *with* them. God could have wiped out the pagan people already in the land all by Himself. . .but He chose to use His own Israelite soldiers. Each one of them could take out a thousand opponents because God was helping them, "just as he promised."

Our battles may be more spiritual than physical, but whatever the case, God will be there too. You plus God equals victory in His time and His way.

THE GOD WHO UNIFIES

There are many people who belong to Christ. And yet, we are one body which is Christ's. We are all different but we depend on each other.

ROMANS 12:5 NLV

The parts of your body work together. Your legs walk, hands grasp, and eyes see. Many parts must work together for you to accomplish things. There isn't a stand-alone part of your body that will make anything happen.

That's very much how God has designed His church, meaning the collection of all people who follow Jesus worldwide. The Lord is a God of unity, and He desires that all Christians—no matter their background, ethnicity, or whatever else makes us "different"—see themselves as one in Him. May we always remember what we have in common—our Lord Jesus Christ.

PURSUE TRUE WORSHIP

And Ezra blessed the Lord, the great God. And all the people answered, Amen, Amen, with lifting up their hands: and they bowed their heads, and worshipped the Lord with their faces to the ground.

NEHEMIAH 8:6 KJV

It is in worship that the Holy Spirit most completely attains the object for which He was given; it is in worship He can most fully prove what He is. If I would that the consciousness and the power of the Spirit's presence became strong within me, let me worship. The Spirit fits for worship: worship fits for the Spirit. It is not only prayer that is worship. Worship is the prostrate adoration of the Holy Presence. Often without words: "They bowed their heads and worshipped."

How much worship there is, even among believers, that is not in the Spirit! In private, family and public worship, how much hasty entering into God's presence in the power of the flesh, with little or no waiting for the Spirit to lift us heavenward! It is only the presence and power of the Holy Spirit that fits for acceptable worship.

GOD'S LAW FULFILLED

The commandments, "You shall not commit adultery," "You shall not murder," "You shall not steal," "You shall not covet," and whatever other command there may be, are summed up in this one command: "Love your neighbor as yourself." Love does no harm to a neighbor. Therefore love is the fulfillment of the law.

ROMANS 13:9–10 NIV

Jesus once turned many people's thinking about the Law of Moses on its head. He stated this in answering a question about the "greatest" commandment: " 'Love the Lord your God with all your heart and with all your soul and with all your mind.' This is the first and greatest commandment. And the second is like it: 'Love your neighbor as yourself.' All the Law and the Prophets hang on these two commandments" (Matthew 22:37–41 NIV).

The apostle John wrote that "God is love" (1 John 4:8) and that anyone who doesn't love others doesn't know God. Clearly, love is important to God, and Jesus wanted His followers to know that we fulfill all of God's laws when we simply love—Him and the people around us.

THE SELF-SUFFICIENT GOD

"But you will not even need to fight. Take your positions; then stand still and watch the Lord's victory. He is with you, O people of Judah and Jerusalem. Do not be afraid or discouraged. Go out against them tomorrow, for the Lord is with you!"

2 CHRONICLES 20:17 NLT

God is self-sufficient. What does that mean? It means that He doesn't need *us*, which is actually great news.

If God needed people to do His bidding, it would suggest that He's too weak to accomplish things on His own. If God needed people to love Him to be satisfied, it might mean that the good gifts He gives are bribes for your affection. No, God is self-sufficient. He doesn't need us in order to be happy, but He enjoys when we delight in Him and His work on our behalf.

So stand still and watch the Lord's victory. Then reach out and spread His victory with your own hands. God doesn't need us to work on His behalf. . .but He delights in us when we do.

GOD'S SILENCE BROKEN

Behold, I will send my messenger, and he shall prepare the way before me: and the Lord, whom ye seek, shall suddenly come to his temple, even the messenger of the covenant, whom ye delight in.

MALACHI 3:1 KJV

There is only one page between Malachi and Matthew. It can be turned in less than a second. But that one thin piece of paper separating the Old Testament from the New spans a gap of more than four hundred years—four centuries of God's silence, without a single word from prophet, patriarch, psalmist, or priest.

When that silence was finally broken, it was pierced by the cry of a baby on Christmas night. And as that tiny voice cried out to be comforted, the voice of an angel was heard saying, "Fear not: for, behold, I bring you good tidings of great joy, which shall be to all people. For unto you is born this day in the city of David a Saviour, which is Christ the Lord" (Luke 2:10–11 KJV).

Joy to the world—the Lord has come!

CLASSICS: CHARLES H. SPURGEON

MASTERING THE ART OF PRAYER

And he said unto him, What is thy name? And he said, Jacob. And he said, Thy name shall be called no more Jacob, but Israel: for as a prince hast thou power with God and with men, and hast prevailed.

GENESIS 32:27–28 KJV

Say what you will of [Jacob], he was a master of the art of prayer, and he that can pray well is a princely man. He that can prevail with God will certainly prevail with men.

It seems to me that when once a man is taught of the Lord to pray, he is equal to every emergency that can possibly arise. Depend upon it, it will go hard with any man who fights against a man of prayer. All other weapons may be dashed aside; but the weapon of All-prayer, invisible though it may be and despised of the worldling, hath in it a might and majesty which will secure the victory. The sword of prayer hath such an edge that it will cut through coats of mail. Jacob was a prevailing prince when he came upon his knees.

"WEARING" JESUS

Clothe yourself with the presence of the Lord Jesus Christ.

ROMANS 13:14 NLT

You wear a shirt, pants, and socks to cover yourself, and these articles of clothing can provide warmth, comfort, and style. Maybe this is the idea presented in the verse above. Take Jesus and everything He has done for you and keep them close so that people can see Him and how He offers spiritual warmth, emotional comfort, and a new (life)style.

This means never leaving Jesus behind. It means never feeling embarrassed or afraid when you have opportunities to tell others about Him. It means letting everyone you meet see who Jesus is and what He can do for anyone who chooses to follow Him. And it means loving others the way Jesus did—sacrificially, with no care about your own needs and desires.

Jesus wants you to "wear" Him at all times so others can see Him in you.

WITH GOD, ALL THINGS ARE POSSIBLE

But Jesus beheld them, and said unto them, With men this is impossible; but with God all things are possible.

MATTHEW 19:26 KJV

The title of today's reading, a direct quote of Jesus from the King James Version, happens to be the state motto of Ohio. It was made official in the fall of 1959 and survived a court challenge from the American Civil Liberties Union in 1997.

It's sad that these six words would be controversial. With God, all things *are* possible. As Christians, we know this both instinctively and by God's Word. But human nature being what it is, we can use the occasional reminder of what God can do. In brief, anything that aligns with His perfect and holy nature.

In the context of today's scripture, Jesus was talking about the salvation of wealthy people. "It is easier for a camel to go through the eye of a needle, than for a rich man to enter into the kingdom of God," He said (Matthew 19:24 KJV). But with God, all things are possible.

What seemingly impossible thing are you asking God for today?

GOD CARES FOR MANKIND

When I consider your heavens, the work of your fingers, the moon and the stars, which you have set in place, what is mankind that you are mindful of them, human beings that you care for them?

PSALM 8:3–4 NIV

Our infinite God boggles the finite mind. In the psalms, David marveled that the all-knowing, all-powerful Lord who hung the stars in the night sky was also "mindful" of human beings—to the point of caring for them.

God made people a little lower than the angels, crowning us with glory and honor (verse 5). We have been called to rule over the works of His hands—flocks and wild animals and birds and fish (verses 7–8). We are actually made in the image of the One who set His glory in the heavens (verse 1).

No wonder David twice sang out, "Lord, our Lord, how majestic is your name in all the earth!" (verses 1 and 9, NIV). As adopted children who bear His name, let's honor and praise God and enjoy every benefit He offers. And let's be sure to make others know how much He cares for them.

CLASSICS: ANDREW MURRAY

YOUR WAITING ON GOD WILL BE REWARDED

The Lord God is my strength, and he will make my feet like hinds' feet, and he will make me to walk upon mine high places.

HABAKKUK 3:19 KJV

The deliverance for which we often have to wait is from enemies, in presence of whom we are impotent. The blessings for which we plead are spiritual and all unseen; things impossible with men; heavenly, supernatural, divine realities. Our heart may well faint and fail. Our souls are so little accustomed to hold fellowship with God, the God on whom we wait so often *appears* to hide Himself.

We who have to wait are often tempted to fear that we do not wait aright, that our faith is too feeble, that our desire is not as upright or as earnest as it should be, that our surrender is not complete. Amid all these causes of fear or doubt, how blessed to hear the voice of God, "Wait on the Lord! Be strong, and let thine heart take courage! Yea, wait thou on the Lord"! Let nothing in heaven or earth or hell—let nothing keep thee from waiting on thy God in full assurance that it cannot be in vain.

GOD DESIRES STRONG FINISHES

*But after Uzziah became powerful, his pride led to his downfall.
He was unfaithful to the Lord his God, and entered the temple
of the Lord to burn incense on the altar of incense.*

2 CHRONICLES 26:16 NIV

King Uzziah started out so well. Second Chronicles 26:4–5 (NIV) says, "He did what was right in the eyes of the LORD, just as his father Amaziah had done. He sought God during the days of Zechariah, who instructed him in the fear of God. As long as he sought the LORD, God gave him success."

Uzziah built up his army and had state-of-the-art weapons. But then Uzziah stopped seeking the Lord. Apparently confident in the power of his weapons, he started doing as he pleased. When Uzziah usurped the priest's job and offered a sacrifice to God, the Lord wasn't impressed. He struck Uzziah with leprosy, and he was banned from the temple.

God blesses those who seek Him. Never let the success He gives blind you to your need for Him. Start and *stay* strong. Be faithful to the God who loves strong finishes!

SCRIPTURE INDEX

AUTHOR INDEX

Glenn Hascall—Days 9, 13, 15, 17, 21, 24, 27, 30, 33, 35, 36, 38, 44, 46, 50, 53, 57, 62, 63, 67, 70, 71, 74, 81, 83, 86, 89, 93, 98, 101, 105, 107, 109, 111, 117, 118, 122, 125, 129, 134, 137, 141, 143, 146, 153, 157, 161, 165, 170, 173, 175, 178, 182, 189, 191, 193, 195, 197, 201, 206, 211, 213, 215, 218, 225, 229, 233, 237, 242, 247, 251, 255, 261, 263, 265, 269, 273, 278, 281, 285, 289, 297, 299, 301, 305, 314, 319, 323, 327, 333, 335, 338, 341, 345, 350, 355, 357, 361

Josh Mosey—Days 10, 18, 29, 34, 39, 47, 55, 65, 73, 82, 85, 94, 103, 110, 119, 123, 130, 139, 145, 154, 159, 166, 171, 177, 183, 199, 207, 214, 226, 231, 238, 245, 250, 254, 262, 267, 279, 286, 291, 298, 303, 307, 315, 321, 326, 334, 343, 351, 358, 365

Paul Kent—Days 1, 2, 3, 5, 23, 41, 59, 77, 95, 113, 131, 149, 167, 185, 203, 221, 239, 257, 275, 293, 306, 309, 311, 329, 347, 354, 362, 363

Phil Smouse—Days 7, 19, 31, 42, 54, 66, 78, 90, 102, 114, 126, 138, 150, 162, 174, 186, 198, 210, 222, 234, 246, 258, 270, 282, 294, 318, 330, 342, 359

Editing by Tracy M. Sumner

POWERFUL DEVOTIONS FOR MEN

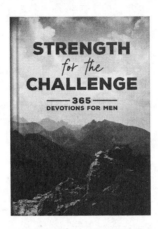

Guys, you know life can be tough. But never forget that God is strong. This daily devotional builds off the inspired truth of 2 Corinthians 12:10, "When I am weak, then I am strong." You'll be encouraged to seek your daily strength from the all-powerful God through Jesus Christ.

Hardback / 978-1-64352-850-2 / $16.99